UNF#CK YOUR BLOW JOBS

How to Give and Receive Glorious Head

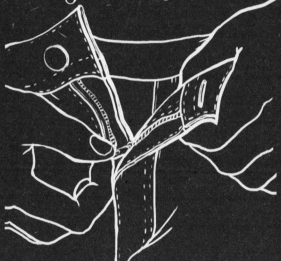

DR. FAITH G. HARPER, LPC-S, ACS, ACN

Microcosm Publishing
Portland, Ore

Unfuck Your Blow Jobs: How to Give and Receive Glorious Head

Part of the 5 Minute Therapy Series
© Dr. Faith Harper, 2022
First edition © Microcosm Publishing, May 17, 2022
ISBN 9781621064589
This is Microcosm #464
Edited by Lydia Rogue
Design by Joe Biel
Illustrations by Gerta Operaku

To join the ranks of high-class stores that feature Microcosm titles, talk to your local rep: In the U.S. **COMO** (Atlantic), **FUJII** (Midwest), **BOOK TRAVELERS WEST** (Pacific), **TURNAROUND** (Europe), **UTP/MANDA** (Canada), **NEW SOUTH** (Australia/New Zealand), **GPS** in Asia, Africa, India, South America, and other countries, or **FAIRE** and **NATURE'S RETREAT** in the gift trade.

For a catalog, write or visit:
Microcosm Publishing
2752 N Williams Ave.
Portland, OR 97227
https://microcosm.pub/writing

Did you know that you can buy our books directly from us at sliding scale rates? Support a small, independent publisher and pay less than Amazon's price at **www.Microcosm.Pub**

Library of Congress Cataloging-in-Publication Data

Names: Harper, Faith G., author.
Title: Unfuck your blow jobs : how to give and receive glorious head / by Faith G. Harper.
Description: [Portland] : Microcosm Publishing, [2022] | Summary: "Penises rejoice! Here is the expert guide you need to the art and science of giving and getting oral pleasure. Learn techniques for causing great pleasure and for communicating desires, needs, and boundaries. Find out the science of why oral sex feels so damn good, work through societal and cultural messages that might get in the way of full enjoyment, and get a good grip on the health, safety, and hygiene stuff you need to know. Dr. Faith G. Harper, sexologist and bestselling author of Unfuck Your Brain and Unfuck Your Intimacy, brings her humor, knowledge, and compassion to help you gain a wonderfully fulfilling sex life"-- Provided by publisher.
Identifiers: LCCN 2021057806 | ISBN 9781621064589 (trade paperback)
Subjects: LCSH: Oral sex. | Sex instruction.
Classification: LCC HQ31.5.O73 H37 2022 | DDC 306.77/4--dc23/eng/20211206
LC record available at https://lccn.loc.gov/2021057806

MICROCOSM · PUBLISHING

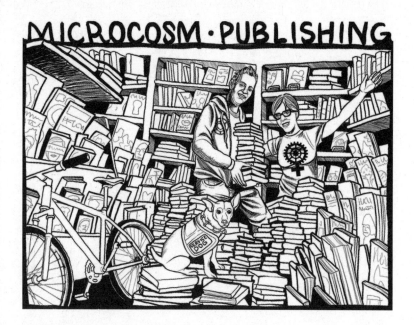

MICROCOSM PUBLISHING is Portland's most diversified publishing house and distributor with a focus on the colorful, authentic, and empowering. Our books and zines have put your power in your hands since 1996, equipping readers to make positive changes in their lives and in the world around them. Microcosm emphasizes skill-building, showing hidden histories, and fostering creativity through challenging conventional publishing wisdom with books and bookettes about DIY skills, food, bicycling, gender, self-care, and social justice. What was once a distro and record label was started by Joe Biel in his bedroom and has become among the oldest independent publishing houses in Portland, OR. We are a politically moderate, centrist publisher in a world that has inched to the right for the past 80 years.

Global labor conditions are bad, and our roots in industrial Cleveland in the 70s and 80s made us appreciate the need to treat workers right. Therefore, our books are MADE IN THE USA.

CONTENTS

Introduction • 7

INTRODUCTION

I've written about intimacy in general and boundaries in general. And I've written about sexual consent and sex toys (sex tools!) more specifically. And this book goes in the same pile with those...unfucking our shitty messages about sex and sexuality so you can reclaim your sexual self and make choices that are well-informed, enthusiastic, and freakin' fun.

Fellatio[1] is nothing more than oral stimulation of a penis. You know, a blow job. Giving head. Slobbing the knob. Whatever. Fellatio comes from the Latin word for "to suck." So if you are reading this book you may be:

- A person who either provides oral pleasure to a partner with a penis (whether one they were born with, one that was bio-constructed, or one they bought at a store and can strap on) or you are considering adding that to your personal menu.

- You have a penis and want to be a better partner when receiving fellatio

- You are a research nerd wanting to learn more in general.

I mean, chances are you aren't lost, and you didn't pick up this book because you thought it was about decorating cupcakes. You're here in hopes of learning more about yourself, a current partner(s), potential partner(s), or human peoples in general.

I should also offer caveats that may or may not be obvious. I do not have a penis. The closest I have ever come to having a

---

1 Verb form is "to filate" in case you need that information for bar trivia night.

penis of my own is when my friend Mei sent me a baculum a few years ago. And while I am an aficionado, I have not sampled all the penes on the menu discussed herein. While that could be fun, it definitely would be time-consuming. And I can't come close to an approximation of delivering manuscripts on time if I'm doing all that as well. So consider this the best advice of a sex educator who has worked diligently to be as inclusive as possible, but definitely is not perfect. And advice contained herein may or may not apply to your real life experiences.

So all that in mind, let's just dive in.

Part One

This is Your Brain on Blow Jobs

*O*ral sex is kind of a reciprocal trade agreement, when you think about it. It's a negotiation between two (or more) people that is advantageous for everyone involved. Some people like a tongue/mouth (possibly among other things) on their penis. And some people like to put their tongue/mouth (possibly among other things) on someone else's penis. And both the receiver and the giver can experience enjoyment, excitement, and fulfillment from the experience.

The word giver is important here. I think the idea that oral sex is purely for the recipient is untrue and part of the shame, stigma, and even mostly-benign snark that surrounds that act. Sex columnist Dan Savage coined the term GGG to mean "good, giving, and game" as a shorthand for the sexual attitudes that are foundational for a healthy sexual relationship. Savage defines GGG as the following: *"Think good in bed, giving based on a partner's sexual interests, and game for anything—within reason."*

This seems reasonable, but is it measurable? Turns out, yes. You won't find research articles that use Savage's verbiage, but you will find a bunch of research on what is termed *sexual transformations.* Sexual transformations[2] are the changes that we make for the sake of our partner or for the relationship itself, meaning *being game.*

Not begrudgingly and eye-rolly but being open to exploring with your partner, in a playful and creative way. Being game means investing your time and energy into something that is an important part of your relationship...and the payoff (sez the researchers) is positive changes in sex, but also other forms of intimacy (cuddling,

---

2 Research nerd alert: This is something that can be conceptualized through a model of dyadic relationships called the actor–partner interdependence model (APIM) which allows for research to be done (like with stats and everything) on the bidirectional effects of relationships.

kissing, etc.), as well as communication and relationship satisfaction in general.

But until pretty far into the 20th century, like the Dr. Faith was alive part of it, oral sex remained something with Roman Empire vibes. In 1950 it was still dead-ass illegal in all 48 states (this was pre Alaska and Hawaii gaining statehood). Likely because of its ties to queer identity.[3] It was something gay men did (e.g., Andy Warhol's movie *Blow Job* [1964] where five different men off screen filated the man on screen). If a straight man received a blow job, it was from a sex worker, not something shared with a GGG partner.

Wanna know who finally got us to shift out of our ancient Roman mindset? The mafia. Seriously.

Mario Puzo's novel *The Godfather* was published in 1969, complete with passages about mutual oral sex between a husband and wife (you know, 69ing). Then the movie adaptation came out in 1972. Additionally, the X rated film *Deep Throat* was shot in January 1972 just a couple of months before *The Godfather* that March (*Deep Throat* released right after in June of the same years). *Deep Throat* was a "blue movie" with a fully realized plot, and it captured national attention and became a cultural touchstone. And? It was financed by members of the Colombo crime family. There is nothing more macho than crime boss shit, right? So as Christopher Hitchens stated in his 2006 *Vanity Fair* piece "As American as Apple Pie" oral sex was "suddenly for real men." It wasn't emasculating to receive or give (!) oral sex.

---

3 Keep in mind there were multiple lies criminalizing queerness. The Supreme Court refused to provide any constitutional protections for oral and anal sex in 1986 (Bowers vs. Hardwick) and it wasn't until Lawrence vs. Texas in 2003 that anal sex was still illegal in 14 states in the US.

All of a "sudden," oral sex as part of foreplay and a common part of people's sexual repertoire became increasingly normal. Even for more vanilla couples. By 1994, Kinsey researchers reported that "27% of men and 19% of women have had oral sex in the past year."

By 2012, the CDC published research showing that among 20 to 24 year olds, "81% of females and 80% of males had engaged in oral sex." And even before that (in 2005), another Centers for Disease Control survey on teens and sexual behavior found that young men and women were performing oral sex on each other almost equally. Meaning oral sex isn't just something that is done to and for men. Thank you Mario Puzo for introducing the larger culture to the idea. And then my millennials? Y'all are responsible for the downfall of crappy chain restaurants and the uptick in tongue stuff. And we thank you for your service.

WHY IT FEELS GOOD TO GET A BLOW JOB

ou've probably heard of MRIs (magnetic resonance imaging) which uses magnetic fields and raido waves to create images of tissues and organs and the like. The cool cousin of MRIs are fMRIs (functional magnetic resonance imaging) which indirectly measures neural activity by measuring the patterns and shifts and differences between oxygenated and deoxygenated blood and how it flows in the brain. fMRI research started showing up in the 90s and quickly became the coolest new cognitive neuroscience tool.

It allows brains to be scanned as we are doing stuff, to see how brain regions light up during these activities. No, this doesn't mean "doing X thing caused Y thing in the brain." Correlation isn't causality, but it is incredibly good information and hugely beneficial in figuring out so much of our hows and whys around sex, desire, arousal.

First of all? The best news is that fMRI data backs up the fact that sex is not addictive in the clinical sense of the word. The American Psychiatric Association (the group of people who look at all the science and determine when there is rigorous enough research for something to be classified as a diagnoses that goes in the DSM) is very specific about what constitutes an addiction. Addictions don't just cause intense cravings, imaging researchers have demonstrated that they *change* personalities, behaviors, our ability to learn and retain what we learned, and how we move our bodies. These are usually caused by substances, which cause significant changes in not just how the brain functions but how it's structured. Only one non-substance causes these same levels of changes, and that is gambling. Not sex.

This doesn't mean that we can't have out of control behaviors about most anything. You have probably done dumb shit that felt very out of control. If not around sex, around something. Sex tends to be a big one though. Because everyone's brains light up during sex. *They are supposed to.*

Even though there are physiological differences in how we orgasm based on our sex assigned at birth, how our brains react are exactly the same. And there is no "sexual center" of the brain, there are more than thirty system areas that become engaged. Our touch processing centers getting activated clearly makes sense. But other "seemingly unrelated" areas like the memory and emotions part (limbic system), the body movement part (the hypothalamus), and the judgment and problem solving part (the prefrontal cortex) all have things to say.

The hypothalamus works to quickly produce oxytocin that assists with enhanced arousal. The logical part (the lateral orbitofrontal cortex) dials way down, in order to dispel normal fear and anxiety about vulnerability while the limbic system pulls up are previous associations with movment and touch and memories about other sexual encounters. This is why, yes, those of us who have trauma histories can struggle to relax into sex regardless of whether or not the initial trauma was sexual.

We also activate a bunch of hormones and neurochemicals. The big ones are oxytocin (which is a bonding/attachment/social safety hormone). And dopamine (pleasure, desire, and motivation). And for my people who are thinking "Hah! Dopamine! Addictive!"

it's important to realize that these chemicals and chemical pathways light up during sex and orgasm, not in similar ways to that of a drug, but in very similar ways to other normal, human pleasurable experiences. Like listening to your favorite song or eating your favorite meal.

Delight is not addiction.

Further, regular orgasms have been correlated with good health outcomes. The prevailing idea is that the extra brain activity and consistent blood flow activation to those regions of the brain.

So why oral in particular?

If you ask 1,000 different people, you will get 1,000 different answers as to why they like what they like. Some people like oral sex way better than any other kind of sex, some think of it as a fun part of diverse menu but maybe not their favorite thing, and some people are just not that into it.

Some people are unable to, for a multitude of reasons, engage in penetrative intercourse and oral sex allows them to imtimately connect with a partner.

Some like that it feels like penetrative intercourse, specifically hot and wet. It may not feel as tight as penetration, but there is the added option of creating light suction instead which can feel great for some people.

Others love the opportunity to be taken care of, the vulnerability of doing so, and being able to focus on enjoying their own pleasure.

Still others like the sounds or the visuals of it. The wet slurping sounds, the humming, and other noises. And the aesthetics of being able to see what's happening in a different way. You are generally positioned in such a way that you can watch your partner engaging in something for your pleasure, which has been described as being akin to watching yourself star in your own erotic performance venture.

And if none of these apply to you? Feel free to mentally insert your own.

WHY WE LIKE TO GIVE THEM

*T*he biggest, realest answer as to why we like to give our partners oral?

It's fun.

Pleasing our partners is fun. Their pleasure can provide us pleasure. Sex is supposed to be an enjoyable thing, so there ya go.

What else?

Going back again to the individuals that cannot have penetrative intercourse or are choosing not to? Oral sex gets centered as our means of partnered sexual expression. Penetrative intercourse, especially the presumed penis-in-vagina kind, doesn't have to be centered as the "proper way to have sex." And isn't it fun to have something else from the sexual menu? And defy all cultural expectations of how we are supposed to have sex?

Anything else? For those of you who want something more science-y or you will be disappointed in my academic database research skills? There actually *is* a possible evolutionary explanation. Authors of a 2010 article published in *Journal of Reproductive Immunology* point out that a multitude of pregnancy problems have been correlated with the pregnant parent's body rejecting the other parent's genes as foreign. The idea, then, is that swallowing the semen of your partner helps your body become accustomed to your partner's DNA thus making it less likely for you to reject their sperm should y'all end up baby-making.

Another study, this one published in *Evolutionary Psychology*, found that when someone perceives their partner as being a "get" (meaning they have competition), are more likely to perform oral sex on their partner to keep them satisfied/less likely to wander off with the competition. The authors of this article, speaking specifically to monogamous heterosexual cisgender couples, posit that it makes it much more likely for men to pass on their genes if the woman in question doesn't leave him for someone who is better at pleasing them.

So sure, maybe. There could totally be some evolutionary benefits to oral sex. Though why things evolved to happen and why we do them now are not necessarily related. Especially since most of us are not in such relationship configurations. "Because it feels good" is a perfectly valid reason to do something.

WHEN THINGS DON'T WORK FANTASTICALLY

*T*haven't met anyone who has a partner or wants a partner who doesn't also worry about sexual performance. Our sexual enjoyment is generally not selfish, but one we want to share with someone else. We don't want our partners to think they are doing something wrong when our bodies aren't responding the way we would like them too. Even though human bodies can functionally derail pretty easily, and it has nothing to do with our partners.

Low Libido and Erectile Dysfunction

First of all, erectile dysfunction (the experience of not being able to get or maintain an erection firm enough for penetrative sexual activity) is super common. Like, so common I really wish we would stop calling it a dysfunction and call it "another perfectly normal, albeit frustrating, thing that human bodies do." Except maybe an explainer that is more pithy and clever than that, so feel free to talk amongst yourselves and get back to me.

How ED is defined and then measured has so much variability, the numbers will also vary wildly. One study said the worldwide variance is between 3 percent and 76.5 percent of people with penes will experience it at some point in their life. Which feels like the scientific version of throwing spaghetti at the wall and seeing what sticks.

Generally, though, the prevailing notion is that ED affects ⅓ to ½ of men at some point in their lives. And while it is associated with increased age and diseases like diabetes, I am seeing plenty of surveys of really young people being frustrated with ED. Like under 30 young. If this is you, you are by no means alone.

Medications That Can Contribute To ED
Antidepressants and other psychiatric medicines:

- Amitriptyline (Elavil)
- Amoxapine (Asendin)
- Buspirone (BuSpar)
- Chlordiazepoxide (Librium)
- Chlorpromazine (Thorazine)
- Clomipramine (Anafranil)
- Clorazepate (Tranxene)
- Desipramine (Norpramin)
- Diazepam (Valium)
- Doxepin (Sinequan)
- Fluoxetine (Prozac)
- Fluphenazine (Prolixin)
- Imipramine (Tofranil)
- Isocarboxazid (Marplan)
- Lorazepam (Ativan)
- Meprobamate (Equanil)
- Mesoridazine (Serentil)
- Nortriptyline (Pamelor)

- Oxazepam (Serax)
- Phenelzine (Nardil)
- Phenytoin (Dilantin)
- Sertraline (Zoloft)
- Thioridazine (Mellaril)
- Thiothixene (Navane)
- Tranylcypromine (Parnate)
- Trifluoperazine (Stelazine)

Antihistamine medicines (certain classes of antihistamines are also used to treat heartburn):

- Cimetidine (Tagamet)
- Dimenhydrinate (Dramamine)
- Diphenhydramine (Benadryl)
- Hydroxyzine (Vistaril)
- Meclizine (Antivert)
- Nizatidine (Axid)
- Promethazine (Phenergan)
- Ranitidine (Zantac)

High blood pressure medicines and diuretics (water pills):

- Atenolol (Tenormin)
- Bethanidine
- Bumetanide (Bumex)
- Captopril (Capoten)
- Chlorothiazide (Diuril)
- Chlorthalidone (Hygroton)
- Clonidine (Catapres)
- Enalapril (Vasotec)
- Furosemide (Lasix)
- Guanabenz (Wytensin)
- Guanethidine (Ismelin)
- Guanfacine (Tenex)
- Haloperidol (Haldol)
- Hydralazine (Apresoline)
- Hydrochlorothiazide (Esidrix)
- Labetalol (Normodyne)
- Methyldopa (Aldomet)
- Metoprolol (Lopressor)
- Nifedipine (Adalat, Procardia)
- Phenoxybenzamine (Dibenzyline)
- Phentolamine (Regitine)
- Prazosin (Minipress)
- Propranolol (Inderal)
- Reserpine (Serpasil)
- Spironolactone (Aldactone)
- Triamterene (Maxzide)
- Verapamil (Calan)

Thiazides are the most common cause of erectile dysfunction among the high blood pressure medicines. The next most common cause is beta blockers. Alpha blockers tend to be less likely to cause this problem.

Parkinson's disease medicines:

- Benztropine (Cogentin)
- Biperiden (Akineton)
- Bromocriptine (Parlodel)
- Levodopa (Sinemet, Carbidopa)
- Procyclidine (Kemadrin)
- Trihexyphenidyl (Artane)

Chemotherapy and hormonal medicines:

- Antiandrogens (Casodex, Flutamide, Nilutamide)
- Busulfan (Myleran)
- Cyclophosphamide (Cytoxan)
- Ketoconazole
- LHRH agonists (Lupron, Zoladex)
- LHRH atagonists (Firmagon)

Other medicines:

- Aminocaproic acid (Amicar)
- Atropine
- Clofibrate (Atromid-S)
- Cyclobenzaprine (Flexeril)
- Cyproterone
- Digoxin (Lanoxin)
- Disopyramide (Norpace)
- Dutasteride (Avodart)
- Estrogen
- Finasteride (Propecia, Proscar)
- Furazolidone (Furoxone)
- H2 blockers (Tagamet, Zantac, Pepcid)
- Indomethacin (Indocin)
- Lipid-lowering agents

- Licorice
- Metoclopramide (Reglan)
- NSAIDs (ibuprofen, etc.)
- Orphenadrine (Norflex)
- Prochlorperazine (Compazine)
- Pseudoephedrine (Sudafed)
- Sumatriptan (Imitrex)

Opiate analgesics (painkillers):

- Codeine
- Fentanyl (Innovar)
- Hydromorphone (Dilaudid)
- Meperidine (Demerol)
- Methadone
- Morphine
- Oxycodone (Oxycontin, Percodan)

Recreational drugs:

- Alcohol
- Amphetamines
- Barbiturates
- Cocaine
- Marijuana
- Heroin
- Nicotine

The other common human experience is low libido. Libido exists on a spectrum. Not just among different people but even within ourselves. Low libido (aka hyposexual sexual desire disorder, impaired sexual function, diminished sex drive, etc) is the mind-willing part of sexual expression. It's about the *wanting* to have sex, versus the physical excitement around of sex (like an erection or lack thereof). The Mayo Clinic notes these signs of low libido:

- Loss of interest in any form of sexual activity, both partnered and solo

- Lack of sexual fantasies or thoughts

- Feeling unhappy or worried about either or both of the above.

This is a well thought out list of indicators because it really focuses on something changing in a way that is not perceived as for the better. It also accounts for someone who is asexual, greysexual, or demisexual. But if it's you and you're miserable about it? It could be the result of many different things. Stress, drug and alcohol usage, not sleeping for shit, other physical and mental health conditions (hormonal changes being a big one), toxin exposure, relationship stressors. One of the other big culprits for both ED and low libido are medications, both over the counter and prescription. Lists of the medications that may cause these conditions are listed below, because that's the easiest fix in the bunch. Speaking to your doctor about changing up your medications may resolve the issue quickly. But if that doesn't do the trick, we are going into a lot of other strategies later in the book that may help, as well.

Medications That Can Lead To Low Libido
Prescription Medications:

- Anti-anxiety medications based on benzodiazepines (Xanax)

- Anticonvulsant medications (such as, Tegretol, Phenytoin, Phenobarbital)

- Antidepressants (including, anti-mania medications, antipsychotics, MAOIs, SSRIs, SNRIs, tricyclic antidepressants)

- Benign prostatic hyperplasia treatments (such as Flomax, Propecia, Proscar)

- Cancer treatments (including radiation and chemotherapy)

- Heart and blood pressure medications (including, ACE inhibitors, a-Adrenergic blockers, b-adrenergic (beta) blockers, centrally acting agents, diuretics, thiazides, and statins)

- Hormonal contraceptives (such as Ortho Tri-Cyclen)

- Opioid pain relievers (such as Vicodin, Oxycontin, and Percocet)

- Steroid medications (including anabolic steroids and corticosteroids)

Over-the-counter medications:

- Antifungals, specifically ketoconazole or fluconazole

- Antihistamines, including Benadryl (diphenhydramine) and Chlor-Trimeton (chlorpheniramine)

- Tagamet (cimetidine)

Recreational Drugs:

This category is harder to listicle, because people's experiences of them vary widely. Alcohol and THC are examples of super-common substances that elevate libido in some people and crash it out in others. So anything you are taking may be having a frustrating impact on your sex life.

All medications operate in the body differently. Time to take effect and time to clear out. So not taking it for one day may or may not be an efficacious litmus test. Read up on whatever you're taking and talk to your prescriber about anything that they have given you. What are options for titrating your dosage or stopping altogether? Can this be done safely? What other side effects might occur that I need to watch for? When would you notice a difference? All that complicated adult-y stuff

Other health issues that can harsh our mellow include:

- Hormonal changes (thyroid hormone and prolactin are two big ones, as are hormones used for bodybuilding and the ones used to treat prostate cancer).

- Medical conditions (UTIs, etc.)

- Vascular issues (anything that affects blood flow, particularly to the penis).

- Other health conditions (diabetes, heart disease, high blood pressure, multiple sclerosis, arthritis, and anything that affects pain and mobility).

- Medications and treatments (chemotherapy, other cancer treatments in general, and many types of antidepressants are the biggest culprits but not the only ones)

- Depression (depression is a total libido killer....50% of the individuals that struggle with MDD have sex drive, sex arousal, and even vaginal lubrication issues), stress levels (cortisol decreases sex drive), drug/alcohol addiction, trauma history (especially related to physical sexual abuse)

- Toxin exposure (ugh, the inflammation)

- Sleep disorders

- A stationary lifestyle (bodies really need to move, and if that isn't part of our regular daily activities, including getting exercise, they get grumpy)

- Body image and self-consciousness

- Relationship problems in general.

Age-related Changes

Oh, my bouncing baby Buddha, save us from the idea that our sexual primes are in our twenties. And praise be sex therapist David Schnarch, author of the book *Passionate Marriage* for challenging the notion by pointing out that there's a big different between one's genital prime and one's sexual prime.

Sure, our genital primes (the physicality of how our bodies function) are when we are younger. But our sexual primes? Not until way later. A study of men in Norway found that those in their 50s experienced more sexual satisfaction than they did in their 30s, even if not everything is as hard, wet, or quick to bounce back, or whatever else we may miss from our youth.

As we get older and have had more sex, we leave behind our exploratory years and enter the years of self-confidence. We know what we like. We know how we like it. We are exhausted of the insecurities that the larger culture has foisted upon us and we started living to be comfortable in our bodies. Which leads to better sexual encounters and orgasms. And if you feel that you aren't there yet? You're literally doing the research to help you get there, which makes you a total badass.

And yes, older generations are still having lots of sex. Even generations that came of age pre-sexual revolution.[4] Because bodies do age and like to do wonky, non-behaving things sometimes, oral sex can become an even more integral part of sexual connection with a partner (read: penetrative intercourse can become more difficult to accomplish for a multitude of reasons). Many older couples related oral sex to a better quality of relationship and overall life happiness than younger people do in studies on sexual behavior.

Due to Disability

Disabilities can be something we are born with (genetic) or something that can happen to us at any time (acquired). In both cases, there may be fuckery to overcome beyond living in a body that isn't performing the way you want it to. The cultural messages around disability (and the presumption that you now exist in the category of non-sexual), are slowly changing, though we still have a long way to go.

Later in this book we are going to get more granular about adaptations that can help you better enjoy your sexual self, but for

---

4 Specifics? Got you, boo. A study of 884 heterosexual couples from the National Social Life, Health, and Aging Project in 2010 found that more than half of those aged 57 to 75 said they engaged in oral sex as did about a third of 75- to 85-year-olds.

right here I think it's most important to note that while individuals with physical disabilities report engaging in mutual sexual activity less frequently than able-bodied folks (especially for folks who struggle with day-to-day tasks without assistance/support), there are many things that predict sexual satisfaction and sexual esteem.

Additionally, the longer we live with the physical limitations of our bodies, the more positive we feel about ourselves as sexual beings. Just like we feel more comfortable with our sexual selves as we get older, we also have the capacity to grow into a level of comfort with our bodies over time as well. Partnered sexual activity focuses more on other parts of the menu and one of the things most frequently mentioned is oral sex.

Which is to say, oral sex is a solution, not the problem.

While on Hormone Therapy

Despite what a neoconservative politician would have you believe, most of the people on hormone therapy are *not* doing so as part of gender affirmative care. Meaning most people on hormones are cisgender. For some people, hormone therapy can be a game changer in terms of desire, arousal, and performance. But because the brain is the biggest sex organ in the human body, our self-concept also has a huge impact on our sexual desire. The entirety of our bodies change with hormones and someone being on hormones for a thyroid condition, as an example, may not feel great about how that changes their physical appearance which can in turn affect arousal.

Additionally? Someone who is on the trans spectrum, and is on a hormone therapy regimen as part of their care, may also notice changes in their arousal patterns and changes in how they perceive their body which impacts sexual desire just as much as it can for a cis person.

Even if you are loving all of the health benefits of hormone therapy, you may find that your erogenous zones have changed which is something important to communicate with a partner.

Part Two

How Our Blow Jobs Get Fucked Up

*W*ell, it wouldn't be a Dr. Faith book if we didn't start here right? The fuckery. If you have struggled with this, or felt anxious, or uncomfortable and not sure why? We might just be able to unravel some of that together.

External Factors and Stigmas

Sex is super important to most people. Not everyone (I see you my sex-repulsed and sex-neutral peeps), but most everyone. While old cranks and media pontificators like to rail about how modern culture has permissioned us to be sex obsessed freaks, that's dead-ass not true. Human beings always HAVE been sex obsessed freaks.

Humans invented the dildo before the wheel. Not just a few years before the wheel, but *25,000 years* before the wheel.

Priorities.

The original dildos were made out of stone (ok, makes sense) and other materials like dried camel dung (please, please don't). But that's not all. It was super openly discussed and shared. Sex and sexy toy usage was depicted in cave paintings . . . going back to paleolithic cave art. Our earliest ancestors were as kinky as we are, bless their hearts.

In his book *Ethical Porn For Dicks*, Dr. David Ley refers to these early images as "petro-porn" (love that) and also points out that these images not only exist across all human cultures, they were also placed in areas where the light of the campfire would cast shadows that would turn the still images into flickering stop-motion mini-movies.

Anywhere humans expressed our daily lives, we all expressed our sexual selves, including oral sex. Cave walls, carved into pottery, in sacred texts (*Kama Sutra*, yes?). Rules of the Roman empire led to new ideas about how power is expressed through sex, which led to ideas that performing oral sex was a service performed by lower caste people to the powerful. David Frederick points out in his book *The Roman Gaze: Vision, Power, and the Body* that performing oral sex was so subvervient it was a disgraceful practice. It was something sex workers offered men, because it was disrespectful to ask their wives for such favors. And men performing oral sex on a woman was even more disgraceful.

Then? The fall of the Roman Empire actually made things worse. It led to a lot of seperatist feudal kingdoms, weirdly segregated populations, and a spread of different sects of Christianity. And? Long-story-short? This also spread new weird rules about sexual acts. Yes, sects killed sex. As certain cultural paradigms changed, criminalization of human sexuality increasingly became the norm. We know that these practices still happened because *most humans have sex.* But ways of experiencing and sharing pleasure that did not relate directly to procreation become increasingly punished (sound familiar?).

Although of course, no one stopped doing fun stuff. And documentation still demonstrates the ubiquity of human sexual expression in all its various forms. While it wasn't shared as something sacred and pleasurable and desirable in holy manuscripts like the *Kama Sutra* anymore (thanks sects), it did show up in association for the punishments levied if people were caught engaging in it.

These documents are referred to by historians as *penitential literature,* documents related to punishments or penances owed for these ridiculous forms of sex that were being done for FUN instead of BABY MAKING. For example, one document from Ireland, specially decreed five years of penance for fellatio (and four for cunnilingus, in case you wondered.)

Hundreds of years of these kinds of laws (which still exist in some areas) and continued struggle with this level of purity culture has created a complicated glop of ideas to unfuck. What we think we are *supposed* to like and what we *actually* like are competing ideas, even to this day.

INTERNALIZED BLOW JOB FUCKENING

*A*s you might expect, alot of our internalized issues with oral sex started with these larger cultural messages discussed above.

But *then*.

We add in our over-worried, over-thinkied, over-anxious brains to the mix and while we may have moved past larger social messages, we still struggle with our own sense of enough-ness.

Meaning, we think other people deserve fun and healthy sex lives, but not us. We're gross. We look weird, we smell weird, no one wants to put their face....you know....down THERE. Most people are aware there is a good amount of research on body image in general, but genital self-image is prevalent enough also to have been studied scientifically. Zero surprise in that how we feel about our bodies overall and our genitalia in particular changes our overall sexual experiences.

Another huge issue for many people is their trauma history. Unresolved trauma, by definition, involves numbness/avoidance followed by hyper arousal and reactivity. Meaning not feeling anything and then feeling too much. And the feeling too much is related to the previous trauma, not current events. And many traumatic events (not just sexual assault, abuse, and rape) are heavily somatic, meaning they create huge swings when it comes to desire, arousal, and orgasm. This can look like being hyposexual or hypersexual, and even moving quickly between the two states regularly.

Masters and Johnson researchers pointed out back in the 1990s (in a study published by the US Department of Justice!!), that the dissociation (disembodiment) that often appears regularly among individuals with trauma histories can be incredibly common in mediating sexual expression. The ability to detach, important to trauma survival, can continue to kick in regularly in our lives. And many people will continue to have sex from this place of detachment, so the physiology of of our bodies is still online but not our emotional states. This allows us to shut off the "this person may be dangerous" part of our brain but also "this is a partner with whom I choose to have a connection" part as well, which definitely can end up being a problem.

All of this is to say, if you notice that you struggle with intimacy, oscillate back and forth on feeling connected and disconnected (with nothing different going on with that partner), or find that it's all fine as long as you are thinking about something else? These may be trauma reactions. And you deserve to heal what is unhealed in you, not just for your sex life but for all aspects of your life.

"You're doing a great job!"

Part Three

Unfuck Your
Blow Jobs

S o if any of this resonates, you are not alone. But the good news? One of my favorite grad school professors once pointed out to me that culture is *anything we create*. We. Me and you. Out there changing the word for ourselves and other people. Let's create a culture in which we get to enjoy what we enjoy and tap out of things we don't with no hard feelings, yeah?

So first things first, blowing doesn't occur (although no kinkshaming if that's what you're into). Using the term blow in association with oral sex rolled in sometime in the early 20th century, with the 1930s, when it first showed up in writing in the memoir *Nell Kimball: Her Life as an American Madam* and then made the rounds in New York in a 1948 poem attributed to W. H. Auden but never claimed by him or his estate[5] as "The Platonic Blow." Blowing someone became *work* the same year, when the comic book series known as the Tijuana Bible depicted McCarthy era politicians discussing giving good blow jobs.[6]

Ok, so no actual blowing. Got it. What's next?

There is no way to talk about it without just talking about it. Just like the only way out of Mordor is through Mordor. Uncomfortable, whether or not y'all are brand new or been together a minute. Though as uncomfortable as it feels, it becomes far easier and more natural with very little time. It's totally ok to throw me under the bus and say "So I'm reading this book that <u>has more information</u> about oral sex than I thought existed on the

5 Which means that there has been no enforcement of the poem as Auden's intellectual property/something under copyright. Which means you can find the complete poem online if you search for it. You're welcome ;)

6 All of these cultural touch points still reinforced the notion that this was back-room, non-respectable stuff, which (as mentioned earlier in the book) took a few more decades to start destigmatizing.

planet. While she probably takes the whole topic way too seriously, I did realize we never have discussed what we like and don't like in that regard."

Because with very few exceptions, your partner is going to know their body way better than you do. And the resounding theme of the rest of this chapter is "Here is an idea....if you and your partner are into it." Meaning, every body operates differently and there is no one right way to give a blow job.

Ok, I take that back, there is. The one right way to give a blow job is to communicate clearly with your partner and then enjoy the agreed-upon plan together.

Other than admitting you were reading this book, how else can you open up the conversation? A lot of my couple-clients (and throuple and so on FWIW) have found using a yes/no/maybe checklist as a solid way of opening up the conversation. But before we even do that, a lot of peeps also really benefit from a from starting with an identity conversation. Not just the "my name is [blank] and my pronouns are [blank]" but getting even more specific to how that relates to their body and their sexual expression. This format is one I modified from a yes/no/maybe checklist written by Tab Kimpton as part of the Khaos Komix series.

Identity Information

- I describe my gender as:

- My pronouns are:

- My gender descriptor words are: (femme, butch, boi)

- My sexual orientation identity words are:

- My sexual role (e.g. top, bottom)words are:

- My terms for my chest/breasts are:

- My terms for my genitals are:

- My terms for my prostate/Gräfenberg spot are:

- My terms for my anal region/alimentary canal are:

- These terms are:

- ___ relatively static for me

- ___regularly fluid for me.

- If they are fluid, this is how I communicate that information to a partner so they know to shift language:

- Some words I am not okay with to refer to me, my identity, my body or, or which I am uncomfortable using or hearing are:

- I am activated (and not in a good way) by certain words or language. Those are/that is:

- Are certain words okay in some settings or situations but not in others?

- How so? (Explanation not required unless you want to, just which situations should be watched for)

- How flexible am I with what a partner might want to call something I like calling something else?

- Any other important information to share?

Yes/No/Maybe Checklists

Great! Next helpful part? Sharing with a partner/partners what you're into. These checklists can be super intricate, involved, and intensive and many of my clients have reported back "Ok, so I'm not kinky at all, considering all the possibilities out there." So trying to create an inclusive one here is pretty impossible. Also, there are really good ones already available, including ones that are more specific to different interests and one that is designed specifically for visual communicators. Some are more specific than others. One is better for visual thinkers and the last one on the list is specific for consensual non-monogamy. Check them out online and see if any feel like a good starting place for you:

- Sexual Interests Checklist (AskingForWhatYouWant. com)

- Yes/No/Maybe List (SexWithEmily.com)

- Yes, No, Maybe So: A Sexual Inventory Stocklist (Scarleteen.com)

- The Super Powered Yes/No/Maybe List: A Negotiation Tool for Sex Nerds (BexTalksSex.com)

- Navigating Consent & Setting Sexual Boundaries: Yes/No/Maybe List (SunnyMegatron.com)

- You Need Help: Here Is A Worksheet To Help You Talk To Partners About Sex: A List For Visual People (Autostraddle.com)

- Poly Yes/No/Maybe List (Polynotes.tumblr.com)

CONSENT

*C*onsent is the informed, voluntary agreement reached for an activity/exchange between two or more sentient beings. When it comes to the expression and negotiation of our boundaries, we generally do so through how we communicate consent. At its most basic level, consent is permission for something to happen. And most importantly, our permission should be punctuated with an exclamation point. In an ideal situation, you aren't having to be convinced, you're saying "yes!" Consent provides a safe framework for interactions. For those of us with trauma histories, a safe framework can be a very healing experience. And, equally important, it allows us to experience own our desires in a sex-positive way.

Permissive consent is what allows us to engage in specific actions in relation to those cultural standards of practice and social norms. For example, originating consent holds that it is not acceptable behavior to stab needles into another human being on the regular, right? But if you go see a tattoo artist, sign their waiver, and pay them for their work, you are engaging in permissive consent.

Permissive consent is our expression of boundaries in context. And despite all our conversations about active, continuous consent the reality is that most consent is not verbal. This isn't good or bad, it's just something to be aware of.

Permissive consent is established in one of three ways:

Explicit Consent: Explicit consent requires the "yes" to be spoken. It is directly expressed consent. A contract that is reviewed, understood, and signed before any exchange is explicit consent. Asking another person "may I ＿＿ your ＿＿" is explicit consent. When we talk about active, continuous consent (meaning active agreement to activity with continued check-ins that the activity is still a go) we are talking about explicit consent.

Implicit Consent: Implicit consent operates on presumptions of nos and yeses. It is the inference of consent based on our actions and circumstances. This isn't a fundamentally terrible thing. We do it all the time. If I purchase a bag of pistachios and leave it on my husband's desk, the implication is that they are there for him to eat. If you apply for a job and your resume includes the names and contact information for references, the implication is that the potential employer will call them to verify your employment eligibility. This is also the area that gets people in the most trouble, such as when someone presumes that engaging in one sexual activity implies consent for another activity that wasn't discussed.

Blanket/Opt-Out/Meta-Consent: These types of consent require a "no" to be spoken. They give the opportunity for the no and if the no is not forthcoming, the "yes" is presumed. This is another common way of operating within close relationships. For example, someone you know well may hug you when they see you and the presumption would be that that is a norm in your relationship. If you weren't down for a hug, you would say "I'm super touched out today, I need a mulligan on the hug" to let them know there was a change in your normal interactions. An example within the BDSM community would be in edge play, where the dom is setting the scene but the sub has a safeword that they can invoke.

Consent is foundational. Healthy behaviors cannot exist without consent being the first part of the equation. But the minute we start saying "I, too, have a personhood to be respected" through the act of establishing and communicating boundaries, we are changing our relationships and our expectations of interactions within our surrounding community. We are evolving toward equity in interaction for the betterment of all humans.

Sample Consent Contract

Since our contemporary conversation around consent started within the kink community, let's look at one of the more formal consent tools that has come from the aforementioned community. Some people may snicker at the idea, but a written consent contract doesn't exist for the purpose of earning extra-woke brownie points. They made sense for BDSM play, but even beyond that, they create a foundation and structure for a conversation about active, continuous consent. And that's not woke-ness...that's badass, thoughtful adulting.

I, _____, hereby declare under penalty of perjury that I am over 18 years old and am not under the influence of intoxicants or medications that inhibit my ability to affirm consent.

I further declare that this agreement is of my own free will and that neither I nor anyone near or dear to me has been threatened with negative consequences if I chose not to enter into this contract.

Both parties agree that this is a private agreement not to be disclosed to third parties except in case of accusation of sexual misconduct by an agreeing party.

If an agreeing party shows or makes public this agreement without accusation of sexual misconduct, it is agreed that they will be liable for damages for invasion of privacy.

By initialing, _____ I agree to engage in all or some of the following consensual acts.

_____

With the following individual(s)

_____

Safer sex methods that I want utilized during these acts include:

_____

At this time I do not intend to change my mind before the sex act or acts are over. However, if I do, it is further understood that when I say the words _____ or make the signal (hand gesture, etc.) _____ all involved parties/partners agree to STOP INSTANTLY!

Signed:_____Date: _____

Signed:_____Date: _____

Disclaimer: This sample contract does not constitute legal advice and is provided for educational purposes only. Check with legal counsel before entering into any agreement.

But What If I Don't Know Enough About Myself To Know What Turns Me On?

As frustrating as it feels to be in a situation where you don't know what gets your engines revved, please know that you are far from alone and you are miles away from unusual. We think of sexual desire as something that someone gives us. That is, it's someone's job to turn us on.

That's an oversimplification of how *contextual* desire really is.

In reality, our sexual expression comes from something within us that we, in turn, can choose to share with a partner. Rosemary Basson's sexual desire model[7] demonstrates that there are several steps that we get to that are about our internal world and our connection to our erotic selves before we get to actual sexual

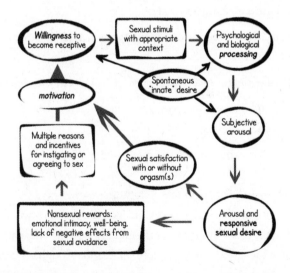

---

7 Dr. Basson's model is an explanation of the sexual excitement cycle of cis women. And while there are absolutely differences among the genders and just within humans in general, I've found that mindset and self-knowledge is important to everyone.

desire. While expanding our repertoire and trying new things and experimentation is also a fun part of being a sexual being, so is slowing down and connecting back to ourselves and what we like and don't like. It's another form of mindfulness. It means being curious within ourselves instead of judgemental. And letting go of the rules and assumptions we have created for ourselves and our sexual encounters.

This all ties to consent as a continuous process, that requires us to listen in to our own bodies just as a continuously. What was right for you in the past and what may be right for you in the future, may not serve you in the present.

Let's look at some questions to help you connect to that space:

1) When did you feel like your most authentic self (connected and grounded in your body)?

2) What things were you doing for yourself that helped facilitate that?

3) What activities give you energy or feel worth the energy they take?

4) What activities feel playful to you?

5) What gets you curious and interested in life?

Engagement Through the 5 Senses

Another way we can build a solid understanding of how we connect to our inner eroticism is by understanding how we most strongly engage in the world. We all explore the world through our 5 senses (or at least as many of these senses as we have access to) and we all tend to be more strongly engaged through one or two of the than the others. In her book *Urban Tantra: Sacred Sex for the Twenty-First Century*, Barbara Carrellas points out that recognizing which sense we most connect to can help us receive with more intentionality. So let's look at where you stand, yeah?

Visual

When you recall details about an event do you most easily go to what you saw? How easily can you visualize your childhood home? Where you live now? What your favorite person looks like? Is how someone looks or how they move their body sensual to you?

Kinesthetic

When you recall details about an event do you most easily remember how things felt when you engaged them with your body? How easily can you remember what your favorite article of clothing feels like on your skin? Picking up a warm mug when your hands are cold? The sensation of jumping into a pool of water? What a partner's body feels like when it connects with yours?

Auditory

When you recall details about an event do you most easily remember what you heard other people say or noises that were made? How easily can you remember someone's tone of voice? How easily do you learn and retain information when it is told to you verbally? Do you most connect with the sounds a partner makes during sex?

Olfactory

When you recall details about an event do you most easily remember what things smelled like? How easily can you remember what your elementary school classroom smelled like? Your favorite flower? Your favorite perfume or cologne? Do you most connect to a partner's scent?

Gustatory

When you recall details about an event do you most easily remember what things tasted like? Can you easily recall the taste and texture of your favorite food? Can you see or hear about something and imagine what it would taste like immediately? Do you most connect with how your partner tastes when you kiss or lick them?

If you are noticing some clear differences in how quickly and clearly certain memories come up based on one of two of your senses, this can provide some great cues on how you connect to your own sexual desire and how you share that with a partner. Practice engaging the world with these senses more on a daily basis and more with a partner and see what new things you start to figure out about yourself!

After Action Report

Any time you're engaging sexually with someone, and especially if you are being game to new experiences, unpacking the experience after the excitement cycle part is over can be incredibly beneficial. Is this something you continue to want on the menu or nah?

Do you feel relaxed? Happy? Calm? Embodied? Satisfied? If this is a person that you have a level of relationship with, do you feel closer to them? These are all signals of a positive experience.

Positivity aside, not everything has to add up to 100 percent amazing. It's also important to ask yourself what you enjoyed specifically...what brough your the most pleasure? What was less pleasurable? What was the most physically intense? Emotionally intense? Did anything surprise you? How so? Was there anything that you struggled to convey in the moment that your partner would have benefits from hearing? Is there anything you wanted to share feedback around?

If you are struggling with some guilt afterward, check in with yourself about whose voice speaks this guilt. If it's external, question that. If whoever speaks with such judgment in your head was silenced (a family member, pastor, society in general) how would you feel? For example, if noone on the planet cared that you liked having sex while wearing an Eeyore onesie, and in fact, were highly encouraging... would you still feel that it was wrong for you? This helps us separate out cultural programming from our own authentic desire.

But...with trauma histories it can be difficult to figure out what is authentic to us, versus the ghosts of past pain. If this is your history, check in with the specifics around that. Did you feel connected or dissociated? Was your entire focus on your partner or did you stop to connect to your own pleasure (because yes, giving is also supposed to be pleasurable)? If you find that you perform well with a partner but struggle with being truly present I'd like to strongly, strongly suggest a therapist who works specifically with trauma because you deserve authentic pleasure, too!

Communication Strategies

Virginia Satir was a therapist and author, often referred to as the mother of family therapy, whose work on resolving communication has been used for decades. She found in her practice as a clinical social worker, that change could be affected fairly quickly by identifying issues with communication and working to improve communication effectiveness.

She theorized that our issues with communication are related to the things we needed to do to survive in our families of origin, which we often carry through to adulthood. This led her to identify patterns in our communication strategies and create a model around them. The first four communication strategies (placating, computing, blaming, distracting) emerge as shields. We aren't being deliberately shitty, we're being trauma reactive and self-protective...even when these strategies no longer serve.

Placaters

Placaters agree. They tend to do things to please others, to their own detriment. The body posture and voice often demonstrate subservience to the person they are trying to placate. The internet often refers to this as fawning behavior.

Blamers

Blamers always disagree as a show of power and autonomy. They may demonstrate intimidating behavior in the process, such as a loud voice/aggressive stance/threatening behaviors. Blamers are the most likely to initiate conflict, but that drive generally comes from feeling very alienated.

Computers

Computers are freakily calm and rational even in in heightened emotional conditions. They strive to be ultra-reasonable which can make them seem unmoving around and dismissive of the feelings of others. A computer is ultra-reasonable, rationalizing and trivializing the content of communication.

Distractors

Distractors don't follow the subject at hand at all. They may seem nonsensical, but they are really working to get away from uncomfortable topics by trying to get everyone to pay attention to something safer. If a topic shift doesn't work, they may ignore questions, drift off, act sleepy, etc.

Leveler

Levelers are emotionally balanced. They are assertive about their wants and needs without steamrolling others. This doesn't mean they aren't emotional, but it does mean their communication is clear regarding their wants and needs and they want problem solving to be beneficial to all parties involved, instead of aiming for some configuration of "you win" or "I win" or "what problem?" Conflict doesn't feel good but it takes less of a toll on their self-worth.

Communication: Noping and Yesing and Feedback Convos

So, clearly the idea is to be a leveler. Satir used the term to describe someone who operates "on the level," meaning with an authenticity and congruence that demonstrates they are trustworthy and engaged. Satir (along with all helping professionals everywhere) demonstrated time and again that we are not our behavior and are entirely capable of recognizing our patterns that no longer serve and adopting new ones.

Leveler communication styles also quickly derail the four more problematic styles quickly because a leveler uses clear language, coming to their point quickly and redirecting back to it when necessary. They ask others to speak for themselves, requests for their feedback, acknowledges their experiences...all without taking on responsibility for anyone but themselves. Levelers address complicated emotions, are responsive to themselves and the people they are talking to, and do not exert pressure on others to follow their will.

Conversations around sex are nerve wracking for most human peoples. After all, this isn't something society encourages us to do. And our extra-annoying narrative around oral sex in particular hasn't helped matters. The only way out of Mordor is through Mordor and the quickest route is to come through with the conscious effort of a badass leveler who goes in wanting to solve the problem, not win an argument.

(When working with couples, I challenge many arguments in my office with "Ok, is this the two of you against the problem or the two of you against each other?")

"No, thank you" to something you don't want to do isn't mean. It's clear. And clear is always the kindest option. If you're struggling with that, I feel ya, and I highly recommend my book *Unfuck Your Boundaries*.

The biggest obstacle to overcome in saying no, and often even to a conditional yes, besides our own internal people pleasing instincts, is to make sure we are differentiating that the no is a rejection of an offer, not a rejection of the other person or your relationship with them. Having a few back-pocket scripts can be hugely beneficial if you struggle to express yourself. Such as:

1) I'm super into you, but that particular activity is not on my menu. It's like shellfish, most people love it and others are allergic.

2) I'm ready to get started. Do you prefer to put on a condom yourself or is it sexier if I help?

3) I can tell you had a long day at work, let's take a shower together and get refreshed before we get into bed.

4) I love how into receiving you are from me, it turns me on. But receiving from you is also a huge turn on and I'd like more of that in our life. Without making it a weird scoring system or something, how can we be more equitable in sexitimes?

The Feedback Burrito

Sometimes we realize something isn't great for us, during or after the fact. This is utterly normal and natural and you aren't expected to know everything and express it perfectly. And you are allowed to realize that something you were game to try is not something you want to continue to do. Or that you still like the idea but y'all didn't do great on the execution. One skill I learned in my doc program[8] was how to give feedback to new interns in a way that incorporated all the things they were doing really, really right with the area that we needed to work on. It's slightly more complicated than sandwich feedback (positive, negative, positive), because the human brain centers negative information so strongly (for survival reasons).

This means taking a little extra care in communicating, knowing that brains can be total negativity trolls, by encouraging while also requesting change. Hence the term *burrito* because the formula is: positive comment, positive comment, place we need to do a little work, positive comment.

Example:

I loved it when you did _____

And _____ was smokin' hot

One thing I think would work better if we did it differently is _____ . I think it would be even better if we _____ instead of _____ next time.

And all in all, I really enjoyed _____.

So, all in all, we are putting the request for something different rolled up with lots of praise.

---

8 From Dr. Heather Trepal. I'm saying that for the sole purpose of embarrassing her by mentioning her in a book about blow jobs with the word fuck in the title.

HOW TO GIVE A BLOW JOB

O k, this is the part you showed up for, right?[9] Tips and tricks for tongue stuff. Sometimes it feels a little silly to write introductory paragraphs for the blatantly obvious, so let's just stoodis. Firsties, though? Anatomy lesson.

Anatomy of a Pelvic Area of Someone Born with a Penis

The pelvic area of the garden variety/no visible indicators of an intersex condition human is just as complicated and wild to contemplate as that of all the other varieties of humans. We don't think of it that way because more of it seems visible but there is still plenty going on on the inside. For now we are going to mostly focus on the external parts, but as we complete these levels we will move into some internals that may be fun for all involved parties. First of all, there is not that big of a difference

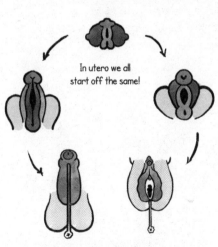

In utero we all start off the same!

How Genitals Develop

9 And I want SO MUCH CREDIT for not saying "the part you came for." Except, whoopsie.

between the genitals of people born with a penis and those born with a vagina, check it:

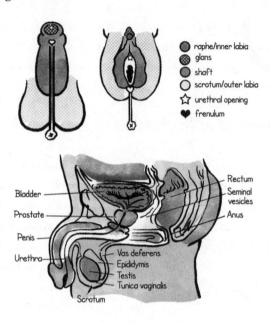

○ raphe/inner labia
⊗ glans
● shaft
○ scrotum/outer labia
☆ urethral opening
♥ frenulum

Bladder
Prostate
Penis
Urethra

Rectum
Seminal vesicles
Anus

Vas deferens
Epididymis
Testis
Tunica vaginalis
Scrotum

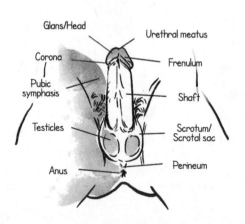

Glans/Head
Corona
Pubic symphasis
Testicles
Anus

Urethral meatus
Frenulum
Shaft
Scrotum/ Scrotal sac
Perineum

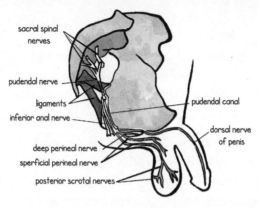

The main nerve that provides feedback and sensation through the penis is the Pudendal nerve. Yes, this is the etiology of the term *pudenda* being used to describe a vulva and yes, all humans have a pendendal nerve that assists in making sexitimes sexy. This nerve starts in the sacral plexus (which is the center of innervation for a good chunk of the lower half of the body, including much of the pelvic area. It wanders down the penis and sprouts off into a bunch of baby nerves through the head.

Most of the sensation in the penis is in and near the head. Meaning, giving good head means focusing *on* the head. And while deep throating can be fun (we'll go there in a minute) it is definitely not required (and the sensations of it can be approximated in other ways). Externally, the head looks like this, where you will be focusing most of your sensory action.

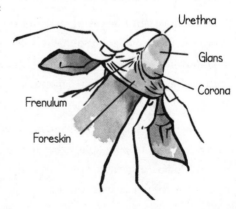

Getting Started

Now for the action part. Even an erect penis is going to bob around like a wind sock, so you want to stabilize the base first. Meaning, you're gonna hold it it in place so you don't get whacked in the nose or take in more inches at a time then you wanted or expected.

This also gives you the opportunity to eyeball and nosesniff for anything in your partner's pelvic region that might be an issue. Sores, cuts, scabs....a not-very-fresh scent....etc. This also gives you an opportunity to apply the condom on them if that's part of y'alls agreement.

Now to stabilize the base, you can use one hand or two hands. As with everything, YMMV, but if you are using one hand you may feel a better sense of control using your dominant hand (the one you write with). If you are using both, try stacking your dominant hand over the less dominant one since that is the hand you will be moving more. As you can see, you get the penis wrangled a bit plus you can do some twisty action with your hands for some extra credit points. Using your mouth and hands together will provide the more intense stimulation than just one or the other by itself.

And since this book is more about the tongue stuff, I'm not going into all the variations of hand stuff. But if you are interested in getting clever in that regard, I highly recommend the book by Barbara Carrelles I previously mentioned, entitled *Urban Tantra*. You get a whole chapter in that regard!

Generally speaking, you are going to want to start slowly. Start by teasing and stroking lightly (but not so light you're accidently tickling them). Alternate using your lips and tongue, focusing mostly on the areas with the highest nerve concentration (the

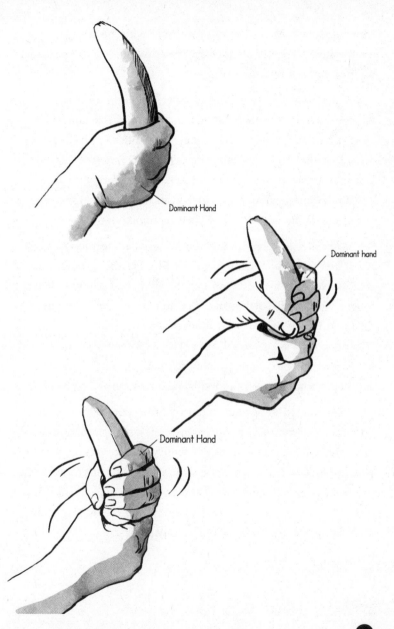

Dominant Hand

Dominant hand

Dominant Hand

frenulum and corona.) You can get firmer with the sensations as their arousal increases and they are closer to finished, rather than wearing yourself out too early.

Make noises of enjoyment, especially if your partner is strongly auditory. Slurping noises and hums of satisfaction will be a turn on to them (and the humming can produce some vibratory sensations that they also enjoy. Remember as you speed up that you want to create and maintain a solid rhythm for your partner. You don't want to go so fast as vinyl on an RPM setting that makes everything sound like Alvin and The Chipmunks, right?

Gag reflex kicking in? Slow back down (and obviously stop ANYTHING you are uncomfortable with), breathe through your nose and let your hands do most of the work. You can make your tongue wide and flat and use it to lick underneath the head (rather than putting the head in your mouth). It's also totally fine to say "Oh my goodness...it's so [big/thick] it's a lot to take in" which is lovely for their ego. Some people find that gag reflex sprays that add a little numbing to your mouth and throat can also be helpful.

Now you are using your hands to control your partner shoving up from underneath you. But what if they start pushing down on your head? First off, rude. Definitely an after-action report issue to discuss. But in the moment if you don't want to disrupt proceedings, lightly grab their hand or wrist, remove it off your head and set it back down on the bed or their lap and say "I got this, just relax and let me do the work" and keep going.

Retrain Your Gag Reflex

Your gag reflex can't be turned off (nor do you want it to, there are tons of things we can actually choke on and die, our gag reflex is designed to help prevent that), but if it's super sensitive you can work to dial it down a bit. You start by placing your finger (pointer finger) on the tip of your tongue while continuing to breathe in and out through your nose. If it's feeling ok, scootch your finger back a bit at a time, pausing to breathe and focus on relaxation skills. Once you hit the point where your gag reflex is kicking in, try holding your finger there while making your breathing slower and deeper and giving it a chance to subside. If it's too much, take a break and start again. If that's still as far as you can go with continued practice, that's just you and your body and we aren't shaming bodies today, ok? At least with this exercise you know where your limit is and can plan accordingly.

For extra sensation, if your partner is into it, you can add some suction by sucking in your own cheeks like you're super basic and taking a super stereotypical selfie.

You can also tap your partner's penis against the inside of your cheek, against your teeth (maybe even some light scraping if they dig that), or against your lips.

Awesome. Fellatio basics. Now let's see how many pieces of flair we can add to this.

Temperature and Sensory play

The possibilities are neigh endless here, aren't they? This is where you can get super creative fairly inexpensively. For temperature play you can incorporate ice, something cold and bubbly (champagne, La Croix, whatever floats your boat since it's going in your

Suck your cheeks in or puff them out to vary and increase the sensation for your partner."

mouth), or something warm and soothing (hot tea is great...mint tea will add a little bit of a tingle). You can alternate between hot and cold as well. For more tingle, you can try an altoid...or if you are looking to get super feisty, one of those popping candies like Pop Rocks in your mouth can be a blast.[10]

You can also use touch based sensory items on your partner's penis, like silk scarves, while you work the head with your tongue.

Auntie Angel's Grapefruit Technique

One of my favorite fun techniques got made super famous a few years ago in the movie *Girls Trip*. Sex educator Auntie Angel (Denise Walker) specializes in fellatio coaching, and her website AngelsEroticSolutions.com is a must visit. Auntie is also a sexual abuse survivor so approaches oral sex from a place of empowerment and reclamation. In this technique, you use a grapefruit (or a decent sized orange) as a penis sleeve. You'll need to cut off the top and bottom of your grapefruit and make a small hole in the middle. Auntie suggests blindfolding your partner so they can smell the citrus but don't know what's coming next, until you slide it over them. You get all the wet squishiness plus the tingles of the acidity in the fruit (and the taste of the juice from the fruit might be nice for you, as well.

Sex Toys! Erm, I mean Tools. Sex Tools!

A lot of people have a sense of unease about incorporating sex aids into their partnered or unpartnered sexual activity. Societal messages (religious or otherwise) often attach a sense of shame to the use of sexual aids, even if sexual intimacy itself is not judged.

---

10 I absolutely had to. It's utterly a dad joke, I know. I'll lace up my New Balance sneakers and go home now, sorry.

But there are many reasons that using sexual aids may be exactly the right thing for you and/or your relationship.

Sexual aids can:

- Be a lifesaver if you're experiencing physical limitations to your sexual expression. For example, individuals who struggle to maintain an erection might find that a hollow core strap allows them to have penetrative intercourse with their partner. Or people with limited mobility can use remote control operated vibrators to masturbate to orgasm, which is incredibly empowering if you have had to rely on others for that experience in the past.

- Be used in a partnership to facilitate increased intimacy and overcome performance limitations with either partner.

- Provide an experience within partnerships that is otherwise out of the comfort zone of one of the partners (such as anal stimulation or BDSM activities).

- Allow people to be authentically who they are. A traditional strap-on can allow someone to participate in penetrative intercourse if they don't have a penis, for instance. Other companies have started producing FTM specific stroker toys, designed specifically to allow transmen the stroking sensation that other men enjoy, while taking into account that they have larger genitalia due to gender confirmation hormone treatment.

- Provide extra stimulation. Some people just need more stimulation to orgasm and aids can provide that without exhausting either partner or having them develop anxiety about trying to please their partners.

- Facilitate intimacy in long distance relationships. There are devices designed to provide pleasure to a partner from afar, such as Bluetooth-controlled vibrators…the best thing for long distance relationships since Skype sex!

- And sexual aids are just fun! I've had many people tell me that they were not in need of any assistance, but when they tried something new (such as a lubricant), they say, "Wow, okay, so much better!"

Probably the biggest question folks have is "will I break my junk?" Meaning, if they use something that provides a LOT of stimulation will it ruin me for what a partner does. Short answer? No. While some people do better with extra stimulation (and you may therefore use things with a partner), you won't stop feeling your partner's touch. If anything, think of it as taking a walk or taking a train. Both have benefits. You can slow down and enjoy the scenery and your own motion getting you somewhere, or you can be less scenic about your journey in order to save time. You get there either way.

We've already talked about using a throat spray, pop rocks, and other such shenanigans. Guess what? Those are also sex tools. They're enhancements you show up to the party with, just like it's a bottle of Cinco and a quart of juice. Except this is edible lube for extra slurpies or whatever.

There are lots of other tools that can be specifically helpful/ fun for oral sex, some of which I'll discuss here and some of which will continue to pop up throughout the book. Like the hollow core strap on mentioned above. Or an erection ring (cock ring) which can help an individual who can get hard, keep blood flow to the area. Or the Elator, which also operates as an external erectile devise with less coverage (just rings and support bars). Or a complete strap on (more on strap-on fellatio in a bit). But also? An open ended masturbation sleeve can provide extra sensation if you aren't into deepthroating and/or don't have the hand mobility (or hands at all) to make a sleeve with your fists.

Sex tools are getting more non-gender specific as society remembers that humans have never ascribed to an immutable binary. Tools like the PicoBong Transformer, which is a sister brand of Lelo, can be used as a massager, a rabbit, an erection ring, a double ended vibrator or a double ended dildo. Like a utility tool for all your household needs.

So consider this big permission to experiment with anything that may help you have more satisfying adventures.

Deep Throating?

Deep throating only means taking the entirety of the penis into your mouth, creating an approximation of penetrative intercourse. It is not a requirement. This is NOT something you have to do to give rock-star head. But if you want to try, many of the other things we have talked about will be super important. Like making sure you have control over depth and movement. Your partner thrusting into your mouth doesn't make them a crap person, maybe they're just super turned on, but you want to remind them that you've got this and let you take care of them. Controlling the position the both of you are in will provide the most support in that regard.

You'll also need to have a good handle on your nose breathing and your gag reflex and your ability to feel in control enough to relax. If you've been practicing relaxing your gag reflex with your index finger, you can practice deep throating with a dildo (another good use for sex tools)!

A little trick for faking a deep throat? Continue to use your hands to cover most of the shaft and move your mouth at the same tempo as your hands so it feels like one sensation. Thennnnn, place the tip of your tongue on the roof of your mouth to simulate the feeling of the back of your throat and let their penis hit the underside of your tongue.

The P Spot

While there is lots of media discussion about the G-spot, whether it exists, etc etc...there isn't a ton of attention paid to the P-spot. Which definitely exists in cis men and individuals assigned male at birth. The p stands for prostate. Which you probably think of as the part of the body that likes to try to kill you with cancer as you get older, but it does have other uses in the body. The prostate is a gland the size of a walnut that lies underneath the bladder. It helps the body make seminal fluid and helps keep sperm alive for baby making and it can definitely aid in having quicker and stronger orgasms.

(Fun fact: For individuals who are needing to ejaculate for IVF treatments with a partner who have erectile dysfunction issues, prostate stimulation is the mechanism used to help them ejaculate. It's called prostate milking and I'm very very very sorry, I don't create the terms I just report on them.)

You can stimulate the p-spot either externally or internally. Externally involves pressing/tapping/massaging the perineum. The perineum is more often referred to as the gooch, grundel, or the taint. The taint being my personal southern favorite...it taint the penis and it taint the ass.

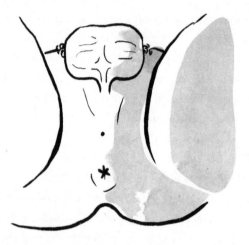

If you want to stimulate it more directly, that requires penetration either with a finger or a prostate massaging sex tool. The p-spot is about two inches up inside the anal canal portion of the rectum. If you have generally average length fingers, that's about as deep as inserting to your first knuckle.

If p-spot stimulation is on the menu, you want to start with light strokes then as your partner's excitement increases, increase pressure for more firmer touch. If you are using a massager, start with lighter vibrations before turning it up to full power. If you or your partner are noticing some mild contractions of their ttesticals or if they feel a little electric-y you are in the right spot.

They can also utilize kegels (more on them later) to help the prostate align against the perineum better for more direct contact.

Dodge, Spit, Swallow, or….The Dribble?

Swallowing is not a requirement. Let me repeat…*swallowing is not a requirement*. It doesn't make you any cooler or better or sexier if you swallow. Not swallowing doesn't have to be disruptive to your partner's orgasm as long as everyone has communicated ahead of time and y'all have a plan.

No matter the plan, having some kind of signal (shoulder tap, whatever) so you know what's up will be incredibly beneficial. This helps make sure you don't take a snowball to the eyeball and you don't accidently disrupt the intensity they've been building to their orgasm.

That's the biggest thing, actually. Maintaining the level of stimulation you have built up to through the orgasm, that is. Not taking a snowball to the eye, unless you're into that.[11]

So if the plan is for your partner to shoot over your shoulder, for example, you can maintain manual stimulation up to and through their orgasm. If you want to swallow, your partner sitting and you kneeling will give you the most control over the experience (yet again). It is more likely to just slide down the back of your throat that way. Makes sense right? If they are laying down and you are bent over them, it's shooting UP into you which can challenge the gag reflex of most anyone.

---

11 No kinkshaming, but semen in the eye can lead to conjunctivitis and possibly even an STI. Including ocular herpes which sounds heinous. Auntie Faith would rather you not. If you get semen in your eye, please flush with water or eye drops. Don't take out any contacts you are wearing until after you've flushed out. Auntie Faith doesn't like to worry about you.

You can also spit into a cup you have by you just for that purpose. Those plastic cups that some fast food places give you that are sorta reusable but not for very long are excellent for this purpose.

Another option is the discreet dribble, where you are holding their penis in your mouth but letting the semen sorta dribble out and down. Sex is already messy so no harm done.

There are endless and creative variations on what you can do with your partner's ejaculate, including kissing them and sharing some of it back into their mouth if you are looking to get spicy.... but, again, none of these are necessary to demonstrate you are sex positive and GGG. I repeat myself not just because I am old and forgetful, but this is a concern that I've had people share with me often. And I promise, some of the most sexually expressive people I know absolutely do not swallow.

But if part of your curiosity is what is in ejaculate?

What's In The Snowball, Anyway?

If your partner produces sperm (meaning they haven't had a vasectomy, etc) that only makes up about 3% of what they ejaculate. The rest of it is:

- Proteins

- Citric acid

- Fructose

- Sodium chloride

- Ammonia

- Ascorbic Acid

- Acid Phosphatase

- Carbon Dioxide

- Cholesterol

- Prostaglandins

- Creatinine

- Minerals

- Calcium

Semen has about 5 calories per squirt, and while reports of it being nutritionally substantive are likely far overrated, it's not harmful and may be a little helpful.

Can I be....allergic?

It is entirely possible (and while not common, is not as rare as you'd think) to have an allergy to semen or an allergy to something present within a partner's semen. This can definitely impact your swallowing choices (and definitely coincides with my encouragement of barrier protection....see further along in the book).

Some people have what is known as human seminal plasma hypersensitivity (HSP) or seminal plasma protein allergy (SPPA), which is an allergic reaction specifically to the proteins found in sperm. It acts like all other allergens, with possible symptoms of swelling, burning, itching, hives, pain, and redness. And anaphylaxis is rare but also possible. Do not fuck around if you have issues with breathing, closure of the throat, swelling of your tongue, etc.

It is also possible to have an allergic reaction to the foods or medicines that your partner has ingested. If you haven't had a reaction to their semen in the past but all of a sudden do, it's worth investigating. Do you have an allergy to a food your partner has partaken in recently? Are they on any new medications? Certain antibiotics can end up in fairly high amounts in the prostate (which contributes to the production of semen), especially the antibiotics that are used to treat prostate infections (ciprofloxacin, trimethoprim, and sulfamethoxazole).

Fellatio Adapted To Disability

The Centers for Disease Control defines disability as "any condition of the body or mind (impairment) that makes it more difficult for the person with the condition to do certain activities (activity limitation) and interact with the world around them (participation restrictions)." So this can include a lot of the different ways we show up in the world. How our brains work (including how they relate to and understand other people and relationships) and how our bodies work. And manymanymany (most) of these disabilities are invisible, or mostly invisible.

Which leads back to (drumrolls and eyerolls please)...having discussions with our partners. The pre-game discussions and the after action reports.

This is anotherf area where sex tools can be incredibly helpful, not just for stimulation but for access. Like a good wedge pillow to help us keep our bodies well supported.

It is also helpful to get creative about positions and communication strategies. Sitting down may be easier for access than lying down, whether you are a giver or a receiver (and, as mentioned above, a sitting partner allows the giver a lot more control over the action). If you use a chair for mobility, there is not a thing wrong with staying in your chair for support.

If you have pain issues, especially if it gets stabby and spasmy, consider that when you are considering positions. Orgasms can increase those sensations along with the pleasurable ones. So if you are fine now but leg cramping happens on the regular, planning to support your legs just in case will make it less likely that it ends up being a complete mood killer.

If your mobility/dexterity can be an issue, don't hesitate to ask your partner for assistance. It's ok to ask them to position their genitals to your mouth, for example. You can also give good head while letting a (trusted!) partner do all of the movement stuff, especially helpful if you have neck mobility issues. You can form a tube with lubricated hands and place your mouth against the tube and let your partner thrust from the other side. While you have less control over their body in this position (hence the "trusted!") you still have your hands present to assist you in not taking more than you can manage.

Fellatio Post-Phalloplasty

A phalloplasty is a bio-constructed penis. Ok, it's more complicated than that in terms of surgeries performed and all that fanciness, but the end result is a penis built for someone's body. This isn't only a set of surgeries that are performed on transmen or gender non-conforming individuals, they are also performed for any number of conditions. Including congenital issues and people with gender dysphoria undergoing female-to-male (FTM) gender confirmation surgery. It's also for those who have:

Congenital (present at birth) conditions, such as:

- Hypospadias and Epispadias, which are both conditions in which the urethra doesn't fully develop, and ends up in a different position on the penis).

- Intersex conditions that have caused significant physical problems that absolutely need medical correction (like aphalia) or where the individual in question is a man and wants less ambiguous genitalia presentation.

- When the penis is just...small. And the individual in question would like it to be larger.

Injury reconstruction, resulting from:

- Circumcision gone wrong

- Car accident or another extreme physical trauma

- Burns

- Explosions

- Penile fracture (typically happens when the penis is bent during an erection).

There are many different phalloplasty options. The most common ones are the radial forearm free-flap (RFF), anterolateral thigh flap (ALT), and the musculocutaneous latissimus dorsi flap (MLD)

RFF involves microsurgery to attach blood vessels and nerves, allowing for the penis to be built around the existing clitoris and all of the sensations to be extended to the full length of the penis. ALT and MLD may or may not be able to accomplish the same thing, but it's dependent on how long the nerves and blood vessels in the thigh flap end up being, a 3D CT scan of the area to look at blood flow can help a surgeon make a determination on donor area choice and success.

Another common procedure is the abdominal phalloplasty, most versions of which do not include nerve connection. The trade off in penis sensation is less risk of urethral complications. While there will be some sensation (it is still living skin, right?) it may not travel the entire length of the penis, and most sensation will come from the clitoris, which (along with the urethra) will remain tucked under the penis. The phalloplasty procedures may or may not include a penile rod or pump (more on that later in this chapter).

Obviously, this is not a book about picking the right phalloplasty procedure, but I would be doing you a disservice by not speaking to the variety of phalloplasty surgical interventions and how they affect sexitimes. Depending on the surgery (and all those other varieties of human response times), it can take up to a year to recover sensation in that area. And it may take several years for the brain to create new maps about these sensations coming from a different place than before (once again back to the brain being the most important sex organ).

The general recommended best practice is for the individual who received the procedure to self-test their sensory responses. This doesn't just mean engaging in solo sex in order to figure out what they like and don't like now (though definitely do that!), but also self testing for sensitivity to pressure, vibration, and temperature changes. Some changes in sensation will hopefully not be permanent. For example, the healing nerves can create some incredible electrical zapping sensations as they reconnect.

The good news is the self-testing can help speed up the healing process, because it encourages the brain's sensory map-making.

Studying orgasm and erotic sensations is so complex, individual, and systems-based that it's really hard to study well. The research that is out there shows that individuals who were able to orgasm before phalloplasty are generally still able to do so, although many report some loss of sensation. Additionally, individuals who were not able to orgasm in the past because of dysphoric distress find they are able to after surgery and their healing period.

And while the enjoyment of fellatio is not incumbent on hardness, being the penetrating partner is. And some people prefer that level of erectness for oral sex, as well. Some individuals end up getting an implanted erectile device. Others may use a sex tool for external support. And others go full DIY, by wrapping their penis in a compression tape like Coban wrap. Since Coban wrap isn't meant to go in a partner's mouth, vagina, or anus, it does need a condom over the wrap, as well.

The general information about erectile assistance after phalloplasty demonstrates that ED medications and/or prostate stimulation are not helpful in the process. However, cis men who got a phalloplasty to correct a birth defect or injury (versus a noncis man who had his penis created completely from another area of skin) may get some assistance from these activities, and it's worth asking during surgical follow-up when discussing being released to sexual practice.

Fellatio After Penis Pump or Rod Surgery

If orgasms were possible before penis pump or rod surgery, they should remain possible afterward. If they weren't before, this surgery isn't intended to correct that issue specifically.

Internal erection support was just mentioned as often being part of many phalloplasty surgical procedures, but are even more common outside of the phalloplasty domain. Current numbers show that there are 20,000 penile implant surgeries being performed each year, a number that includes cis men and non-cis individuals. More information on options is included later in this book, on the assistance with erectile dysfunction section.

Fellatio on a No-Op Trans/GNC Partner with a Penis

The prevailing "wisdom" (read: presumption) is that hormone therapy as a gender confirmation treatment led to hyposexuality. And turns out? Not true. Trans women have the same rates of hyposexual desire disorder as cis women.

Knowing that the the glans of the penis and the clitoris have the same point of origin in utero (see earlier in this book) can be helpful for a trans woman or transfemme individual who enjoys oral stimulation but is also experiencing dysphoria. But if glans stimulation feels like too much, try the trick from Allison Moon's *Girl Sex 101* which is to move down about an inch from the glans on the dorsal section (the underside) of her genitalia. As seen in the anatomy images earlier in the book, there is still a lot of nerve ending to stimulate while being less likely to overstimulate your partner (in the painful ow kind of way, instead of the fun way). My book *Unfuck Your Cunnilingus* also goes into considerations that would fall into the cunnilingus category, even when performed on a no-op partner with a penis.

Also? Some individuals who have been on estrogen for a while start to notice that their erections are softer, making penetrative activities more difficult. Oral sex often works just brilliantly if you're down.

Fellatio Post Metoidioplasty

A metoidioplasty is a gender confirmation surgical technique where a penis is created for a trans man or transmasc individual. It's created primarily from the tissue from their existing clitoris, which has enlarged from hormone therapy. The three general types of a metoidioplasty are the simple one (where the suspensory ligaments surrounding the clitoris are released, so they are no longer holding the erectile tissue close to the inner labia). A full metoidioplasty is generally understood to include not just that ligament release but urethral lengthening, a urethral hook-up (where the two ends of the urethra are now attached), and testicular implants. Finally, a ring meta includes the creation of a whole new urethra using skin from the labia, which allows the individual to urinate standing up.

Once again, this isn't this isn't designed to be a decision making guide for individual surgical needs, but to demonstrate the huge variety of options out there. There is no "I have a new partner who let me know they have a meta so now I know what to do, it's all good." A successful surgery can still have extensive recovery times and experimentation regarding different sensations. Some people experience less firm erections due to the cutting of the suspensory ligaments, and may benefit from an ED medication and/or pumping (more on that in a bit) and may require some creativity with barrier methods (more on that, as well, in a bit).

Fellatio with an Intersex Partner

It is actually really difficult to identify the difference between intersex and perisex people. We all have stronger and weaker expressions of the different characteristics we term male and female. That being said, the prevailing statistic is 2%. 2% of people have hormones, chromosomes, and/or physical anatomy that varies from our traditional understanding of biological sex. Which also means most intersex people are not going to present with visible anatomical differences to a partner, but they may have different concentrations of hormones affecting their desire rates, their sensitivity, their ability to achieve and maintain erectile tissue, etc.

If your partner has visible anatomical differences, the most important thing for you to know is that you're still going to be focusing on erectile tissue in one place. Remember all that stuff about the penis and clitoris developing from the same organ system? The term for that is homologs, so you can have one or the other or something in between but not both a penis and a clitoris. So when you see news stories about someone who is intersex having both male and female sexual organs? Clearly not just wrong but biologically impossible.

When we are talking about visible differences, and characteristics of both sexes, we are talking about a body that looks like one of the following:

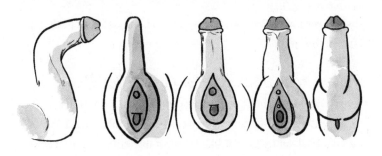

And just like this book is not intended to be a "choose your own surgical adventure," it's also not to be an Intersex 101 guide. But it is a fellatio guide! And since bodies come in many variations it's important to honor that and think about how we share sexual pleasure with partners of our bodies right? So we want to discuss with a partner where and how we want to be touched. Where are our sensitive areas? What feels good and what feels less good? And these questions remain true for all bodies, not just for partners with a natural body variation. And if they do have a natural variation there may be other information to consider. For example, are they interested in any penetration of their vaginal canal? They may not have a fully developed vaginal canal, more of a pouch in that area (vaginal agenesis) which could lead to sensations that are uncomfortable or even painful. Also knowing their surgical history will be important. Many individuals with visible variations are operated on when they are very young without their consent by panicked doctors and family members. They may have scar tissue to contend with and/or medical trauma surrounding that area of their body that you will want to be aware and respectful of.

And just like with any other partner, you will want to have discussions about disease transmission, and yes we are going to discuss getting clever with STI protection and different body types later in this book!

Fellatio with a Strap On or Convertible Packer

A strap-on is a synthetic penis that someone can wear with a harness or specially fitted undergarments. A convertible packer (usually called a pack-and-play just like the portable cribs) is a packer that can be bent up to an erect state for sexitimes.

There are full penis strap ons to be worn by individuals who do not have a penis, and there are the hollow-core strap ons (mentioned earlier in this book) designed to be worn by someone who does have a penis but doesn't achieve a strong erection and wants more stiffness...therefore they fit their biological penis into the hollow part of the strap on.

Why are we talking about store-bought options? Because a blow job is a blow job is a blow job. I don't care if someone's penis developed in utero, was bio constructed by a lovely surgical team, or purchased at the Love Shack Boutique.

Strap on / erect packer blow jobs can have multiple meta-intents beyond the obvious sexual pleasure. They may be used realistically (this is my penis and this is fellatio of my penis) or they may be used as part of a BDSM scene (it's a mechanism of playing power-dominance-control, the fellatio itself is a tool) or part of a genderfuck scene (again, the fellatio is a tool used to disrupt normative paradigms).

And the biggest question people tend to have about strap-on / erect packer fellatio is does it feel good for the receiver. Answer? Yes. The visuals aspect of fellatio is a huge part of the turn on (as mentioned way earlier in this book). Plus, the base of the toy sits against the genitals of the person wearing it, which provides sensation. Additionally the design of the harness itself (for strap-ons) can provide extra stimulation (a strap that runs down the middle of one's genitals can provide extra sensation) and there are also strap-ons that vibrate at the base.

Plus you can still use your hands to provide extra stimulation of their body while your mouth does its job. And that part of the experience will be a huge part of your conversation around it. What aspects of the experience feel best? How else (if at all) do you want to be touched or stimulated? Strap-on/erect packer fellatio allows you both to be in a different playful and experimental space.

One consideration for the giver to consider is that a strap-on may be more irritating to their throat. The density of different materials may affect you differently, and you can't really tell by looking/touching a sample at the sex toy store. And you definitely cannot deep throat the floor sample to see how it feels right? Consider that your tolerance for width and girth may be different, and you may want to use something that is more smooth (versus something ridged for penetrative experience). And also plan to care for your mouth and throat tissue the same way you would after yelling at a football game or singing in a choir all day!

How to Receive a Blow Job

*B*eing a polite receiver is about consideration and communication. What can you do to be a considerate receiver right off the bat and how do you figure out the rest? There are definitely some thou shalt nots to keep in mind, though all thou-shalt and thou-shalt-nots are also *situationally dependent*. Maybe your vibe with your partner includes a little kink play that involves something that would otherwise be a default no. Have fun in that space as long as everyone knows what the scene includes.

- Thou shalt not ignore thyne hygiene. Presume that a day at work and a sweaty bike ride home did a number on your pito and your naglas. Even if you don't smell it, someone's face down there definitely will. Err on the side of caution and freshen up for sexitimes.

- Thou shalt consider some trimming as well. Pubic hair protects sensitive skin (and also serves as increasing surface area of your body for releasing hormones. But a lot of pubic hair can get in the way of partnered shenanigans. Getting yourself some inexpensive clippers and using a guard on them so you don't buzz yourself itchy bald is generally considered good manners. Bonus? Your chihakchin will look bigger in a tighter nest.

- Thou shalt not shove someone's head down onto you. Enough said?

- Thou shalt have a plan for ejaculation. Is your partner comfortable with swallowing? Or do you need a duck-and-dodge signal? Or a spit cup? Is a certain position easier for your partner for swallowing (them kneeling while you sitting tends to be an easier position for swallowing without choking).

- Thou shalt consider the foods you eat. Semen can taste and smell pretty gnarly and a lot of that is related to food. That more musky/bitter vibe can come from a lot of different foods, but the biggest offenders are garlic, onions, cruciferous veggies (broccoli, cabbage, leafy greens, asparagus, etc.) and meat and dairy products. Foods that make semen a little less alkaline, therefore less bitter, include: celery, parsley, wheatgrass, warming spices (like cinnamon and nutmeg), and higher enzyme fruits (like pineapple, papaya, and oranges).

- Thou shalt discuss if your receiving is supposed to be a warm up for other activities or if you are meant to return the favor. Being able to languish in enjoyment is totally fine as long as your partner is good with giving without expectation of immediate return.

- Thou shalt make eye contact, be complimentary and gracious and grateful. And anything that didn't go well is discussed carefully and possibly with a feedback burrito.

Being a thoughtful and grateful receiver doesn't just make you a nice human, it will earn you lots of respect and, quite likely, lots more future head. Worth it!

Emotional and Medical Concerns

Earlier in the book we talked about how things can change due to different circumstances and times in our lives. Whether for the better or for the more frustrating, different means making adjustments. This part of the book is designed to be as granular as possible around a lot of these options.

Adapting to Your Body

While a lot of this chapter is about adapting our bodies, I want to start with slowing down and caring for our bodies first. It may not change anything about how your body sexually responds, but it will definitely change your relationship with that response. And time spent on caring for your body and your health in general is never wasted, trust the clinician nutritionist.

Where Does Desire Come From?

Whenever I am working with anyone on their issues surrounding intimacy, I start by reminding them that sexual desire is something that is within us that we then choose to share with a partner. Sexual desire isn't something somebody else gives us. Even if they are smokin' hot (Paul Rudd, call me!).

One of the first things we do is figure out what helps them feel most in tune to their own sexual selves. Do they feel better when they have time to work out, when they eat a certain way, when they get a day to themselves to rest and not answer emails? This self-care based on self-knowledge work is foundational to everything else.

So let's start there:

• When in your life did you feel best in your body?

- What supported that experience for you?

- What would help you reclaim that in the present?

- What can you start doing this week?

Pleasure Mapping

Sex educator Kenneth Play uses the term *pleasure mapping* to describe the process of connecting to how you enjoy the sensations of your body. This is another level in from connecting to your innate sexual desire, plus creates space for creating and intensifying new erotic pathways.

Because one of the coolest things about having a human body, is how readily the brain creates new sexual stimulation pathways. We think of pleasure and orgasm as depending on the stimulation of our genitals and research continues to show that's clearly untrue.

Brains are creating new neural pathways all the time, and remapping your senses in order to achieve sexual satisfaction through other parts of the body and in other ways. And if I was reading this right now, I would be thinking "ok, so how the fuck do we do that?" so I imagine you are, too. While my book *Unfuck Your Intimacy* goes into detail about sensate focus exercises, this is actually really different. Where sensate focus is about connecting to the joy of touching your partner's body, pleasure mapping is about connecting to the joy of being touched by others.

Try slowing way down with your partner and pay attention to how and where your body responds:

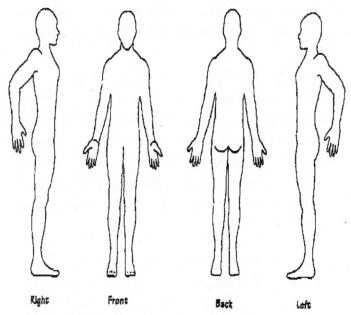

Right   Front   Back   Left

- What kind of pressure do you enjoy?

- How intense?

- What kind of rhythm and movement?

What positions are you most comfortable in? What about what position your partner is in?

Is there anything else you noticed?

Stress Management

While we all know a few stress divas who seem to have a homing beacon for inviting stress in, most of us don't choose stress, we just have to deal with it. Stress is our sense of overwhelm or struggle to cope with the mental/emotional aspects of pressure in our lives. Whether it's everyday stress, life events stress, or disintegration of society stress, this is the shitshow we've been handed. And research shows the more we try to avoid stress, the worse it gets. So what does help?

There's good news, I swear there is good news. Research supports that we have far more control over our experience of stress and how it affects our bodies than you'd think. Not by chucking everything and living in a van down by the river, but by changing your perception of stress.

Some smart people compared the National Health Interview Survey data to mortality data in the US. They found that stress alone isn't so bad for you.

Embracing Stress Through Mindset Training

The author of the book *The Upside of Stress*, Kelly McGonigal, (whose research is the starting point for a lot of what I write about here) states: "Embracing stress is a radical act of self trust."

We've been told not to though, haven't we? We're told to avoid stress, to calm down, that it isn't good for us. Harvard Business School professor Alison Wood Brooks asked hundreds of people the same question: If you are anxious about a big presentation, what's a better way of handling it? Feeling excited or trying to calm down?

91% of people said "try to calm down."

But the stress isn't in and of itself bad—it's not necessarily a problem you need to solve or get away from. This is borne out by multiple studies, including the one mentioned above, where the researchers found that just saying "I'm excited" out loud can reappraise stress as excitement. Despite what most of us have been told, it's easier for the brain to jump from anxious feelings to excited ones rather than calm ones. Cortisol is going to be activated because something matters to you. But you can consciously label it as excited instead of stressed, which changes how you interpret and experience your own body.

The practice of reframing our thoughts from those of overwhelm to those of empowerment is known as mindset training. Mindsets are really nothing more than the beliefs we have about ourselves and the world that shape our realities. This isn't negating the fact that we may be dealing with really fucked up situations, but is about taking back whatever power we have in our own responses when dealing with shitshow scenerios.

One of the biggest predictors of stress overwhelming us is our perception of not being up to the task, so focusing on the fact that we are, indeed, up to it shifts our thinking.

It's super important that you don't beat yourself up for not doing stress well. The entire engine of modern society operates on the psychic energy of people not doing stress well. The whole game is designed to work that way. If you are exhausted, burned out, depleted, experiencing adrenal fatigue, and the like, just changing your mindset isn't going to resolve all that.

It took years if not decades to get you to the point of exhaustion you are sitting at right now, right? You can't unfuck this level of attack on a human body by chanting "I'm not stressed, I'm excited!"

Any stressful situation can become an opportunity to practice a mindset shift. When you notice your stress response activating, you can remind yourself that your body is reacting to something because it's important to you. Then, use that energy to help carry you through the situation. Whether you are getting through a stressful interview or fighting facism, being alert, engaged, and present is vital to success.

Mindset training seems awkward at first, but once you build that neural pathway it becomes more natural and more likely to be your automatic response. As you practice, you won't have to work so hard at it over time. Your stress mindset will also change how you react to others' stress. Mindset leads to resilience. And emotional resilience is one of the first lines of defense against mental illnesses like depression and learning what behaviors build that up could clue physicians in on how to treat those illnesses.

Having a GOOD Mindset

You can practice mindset training as part of your daily self-care routine. I like the GOOD acronym of mindset training since it doesn't involve any kind of fake hype about shitty situations, it really just is about being grounded in your own self-efficacy. And clearly you are a fucking survivor—you're reading this right now, which means your survival rate thus far is 100%, right? This is one of those internal work exercises that might be easier to make external by journaling through it, especially at first while you get used to the process. But I am, for once, not insisting you write everything down if you really hate that shit!

Gratitude: Focusing on gratitude is a really good part of our mental health in general and can create a perspective shift in our day. This doesn't mean discounting what's problematic, but focusing more on what's good in your life.

Openness to Possibilities: If we are gratitude focused, we are far more likely to be aware of solutions, support, and opportunities around us. In a negative mindset, we are more likely to dismiss things that are available to us (or not notice them at all) because we are overwhelmed and frustrated with life in general.

Opportunities in this Experience: No matter what experience we are having, we can focus on the opportunities that exist to help us grow. We can learn more about different situations and ourselves even if we don't achieve the success we were hoping for. As someone who does a lot of political advocacy work, I can tell you that every lost battle taught me a new strategy of approach for next time.

Determine: Visualize yourself successfully embracing the challenges ahead. This is hardiness in action. If you mentally set yourself up for success, you are in the right frame of mind to tackle the project. And no, you aren't more frustrated if things don't go perfectly. I've found that even when I don't succeed, I'm still proud of myself for going in prepared and positive because I feel like I really gave it my all.

Nutrition and Environment

While there is no magical erectile dysfunction dietary formula, I've worked with a lot of people who have created significant improvement in that area by decreasing their processed food intake, adding whole food supplements and/or quality herbs, and even experimenting with their bodies' responses to electromagnetic fields.

I know this all sounds super suspicious, like I am now going to try to sell you on some weird product package that costs thousands of dollars. Actually the opposite is true. Small dietary changes can have a huge effect and (apart from the fact that better quality food costs more) it's free to try. Turning off wireless in your house and/or putting your phone in airplane mode while you sleep? Free to try. And you don't need wifi access when you're conked out anyway.

Good quality supplements can be (ok, are) more expensive but can also be incredibly helpful. Typically I look at supplements that support the body's sex hormones (tribulus, ginseng, selenium) and response to stress (adaptogenic herbs like rhodioloa, ashwaganda and the like).

If this route is more your speed, it really is of benefit to consult with a nutritionist who works in this area for an individualized plan. So often people say "just give me a meal plan and tell me what to take" and there are so many more personal factors at play. I like looking at individual symptoms and labwork if it's available. Sometimes there is something going on like a zinc deficiency that is having a cascade effect throughout the body and is easily corrected.

Kegels

Being healthy is far easier if we exercise, right? Sexual health has its own exercise...the Kegel. Obviously, Kegels aren't magically curative for all kinds of sexual disorders but they are one of the go-to exercises that really help a lot of people! Kegel exercises are designed to strengthen the pelvic floor muscles, focusing specifically on the "PC" (pubococcygeus) muscles. Kegels have tons of practical use for all kinds of issues, whether you have a vagina or penis.

Dr. Arnold Kegel was a gynecologist who developed these exercises for people who had pelvic floor weakening post-childbirth. He found another interesting side benefit: His patients who were doing kegels regularly were achieving orgasm with greater ease and frequency, and had a more intense experience, showing that kegels have an additional benefit to sexual intimacy. They have been found to help both women and men better achieve orgasm, and can help both sexes feel more in control of their sexual experience for a few reasons:

- Kegels help control urinary incontinence, so many individuals feel more secure during sexual activity and less likely to leak urine.

- Kegels help give the individual on the receiving end of penetrative intercourse more control over the experience and more intense orgasms. They also create a tighter vagina or anus, therefore increasing the pleasure of the penetrating partner as well.

- Kegels help bring more blood flow to the pelvic region in women and the perineum region in men, potentially intensifying your arousal.

Kegels can be done with or without an aid (such as a dildo, vibrator, or tool designed specifically for kegel mastery like Betty Dodson's kegelciser). They can be done solo (which is usually a good place to start) as well as during penetrative intercourse (which can be a lot of fun for both partners).

Here's how to do them:

- Locate the muscle group in question by squeezing the muscles you use to stop your urine flow. If you are urinating and are able to halt the flow, you have the right muscle group. Your stomach and buttocks muscles should not tighten in the process. You also don't want to do your kegel exercises when emptying your bladder on a regular basis. That can lead to weakening the pelvic floor muscles which can prevent you from fully emptying your bladder (which, in turn, can lead to an increase in urinary tract infections).

• If you are using a kegel aid, lubricate the aid before insertion and practice kegels lying down. If you are not using an aid, it may be of benefit at first to practice lying down.

• Squeeze the muscle group for three seconds, then release for three seconds. Complete 10 to 15 cycles of squeeze and release.

• Try to do this at least three times a day. The more regularly you perform the exercise, the better results you will get (just like any exercise).

As you get more comfortable doing this, you will find that you don't have to set aside "kegel time" to be effective. You can do them while engaging in other activities since no one will know what you are up to—unless of course you are doing them during sex, in which case your partner will know and appreciate it!

Medications for Erectile Disfunction

The most common cause of erectile dysfunction is problems with blood flow to the penis. Hardening artieries mean less hard penes, as do high blood pressure, cholesterol issues, a variety of neurological conditions (including chronic lower back pain), and mental health issues like depression and anxiety. If you are treating all of those underlying health concerns and still not getting the vibe you want?

The first medical line of treatment for erectile dysfunction is medications. You know. The little blue pill and its cousins. You're eating right, moving your body, eating brazil nuts for the selenium, etc., and still unhappy with your body's sexual excitement responses? These medications are generally effective without a ton of side effects.

If you've been curious about how these medications (avanafil, sildenafil, tadalafil, and vardenafil) work? It's by enhancing the body's own nitric oxide which relaxes the muscles of the penis, which helps support blood flow in the region which is necessary for getting an erection.

This is why these medications are generally more effective for treating ED than testosterone replacement therapy (TRT). There is some connection between ED and low testosterone, but it's not a simple or well understood one. There are plenty of people who have ED who have testosterone in a normal range...and there are plenty of people with low T that still have erections that turn corners. But if your testosterone is low, TRT may help your ED... and it will quite likely help you feel better in general, which will help your libido, which will help everything else.

But if these options don't do the trick?

Surgical Options and Penile Implants

While it seems like a pretty rare intervention, it turns out that approximately 20,000 individuals per year opt for penile implant surgery. And research conducted by individuals in the Duke Division of Urology found that 90% of surgery recipients studied were very happy with the results, would have the surgery again, and would recommend it to a friend. So clearly this all bears discussion.

For the zillionth time in this book, all this information is presented as options that you can discuss with your doctor, not a decision guide or encouragement of any particular intervention. This is, clearly, a more substantive intervention than managing stress and doing kegels, right?

Implants are placed completely inside your body, versus a sex tool that you use and remove. This surgery does mean that you wont have a "natural" erection anymore and therefore is designed as an option when all others have been exhausted. The consensus from doctors about the ability to orgasm is that if you could before, you should continue to be able to after healing from the operation (about two-ish months).

But this isn't an orgasm-enhancing procedure, it's an erection firming one. The implant works by replacing the spongy tissue that maintains the blood flow within the penis (the corpora cavernosum if you're curious....and I know you are, you big nerd). It's something that has to be prescribed, though that means that insurance companies do often cover it (yes, including Medicare). And there are three main options:

Implanted Rod
The implanted rod is exactly what it sounds like it would be. It's the easiest procedure, the least expensive procedure, and is totally concealed in the body. Because there are fewer mechanical parts, they last way longer as well, like up to 20 years. It works simply: to

be erect you bend the penis into the erect position and when you're done, you bend it back down. So that's the biggest "issue" with the implanted rod, you always have a semi which may feel and look awkward.

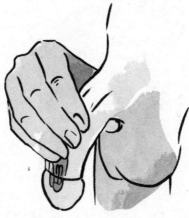

2 Piece Inflatable Pump

With this option, there is a pump that is tucked into the scrotum that pushes a saline solution that is held in the same area up through the cylinder implanted in the penis. Filling the cylinders creates the firm erection. How it works: Gently squeeze the concealed pump in the scrotum several times. This moves the saline solution from the reservoir into the cylinders. As the cylinders fill, the penis becomes erect and firm. To end the erection, gently bend the penis down for 6-12 seconds. This transfers fluid back into the reservoir.

This pump is simpler than the three part pump, and unlike the rod, isn't as evident through clothing. It's also the cheapest option on the market. It does require some dexterity with your hands and the pump itself is more noticeable. Not painful or sharp, but a little more janky than the next option which is considered softer.

The three part pump is like the two part, except it has a third (doh!) component intended to help the deflation process, which is also in the scrotum...so you don't have to bend the penis itself so it is easier on your natural tissue. It is easier to inflate since it is larger and softer and provides better rigidity for the same reason. The downside is that because there are more components to deal with, there is also a higher failure rate. In some parts of the world, the 3-piece pump has been discontinued because of the failure rate (50% in one European study). And for some people it can last up to 15 years before needing replacement, for others it may need replacement after just a few, which is a big YMMV consideration. It's also the most involved and most expensive of the surgical options.

Chordee Surgical Correction

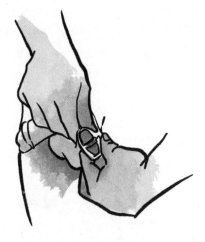

Since we are talking about surgical options, it's also important to recognize that sometimes erections are happening just fine but are super painful. Now many penes have curves, but a painful bend, especially nearer the tip, is a sign of a developmental wonkiness that can only be corrected through surgery. This can occur with hypospadias (which is where the urethra doesn't develop to the tip of the penis, and lands somewhere on the underside) or without, where there is just more elastic tissue development on the top half of the penis than the bottom half, or significant scar tissue develops in or around the urethra.

Generally hypospadias is noticed early on and is surgically corrected, but not always. And non-hypospadias chordee may not be noticed until adolescence or adulthood, when the individual notices that erections are painful or not as strong as desired. Surgical correction is the only course of treatment for chordee with or without hypospadias (and depending on the severity could require more than one procedure. But the surgery can provide signficant pain relief (sex shouldn't hurt unless that's what you're into!) as well as help with erections and orgasming. It is generally done as an outpatient survey, though you may need to wear a catheter for a few days while your penis stays wrapped to avoid swelling.

STI PREVENTION AND SAFETY

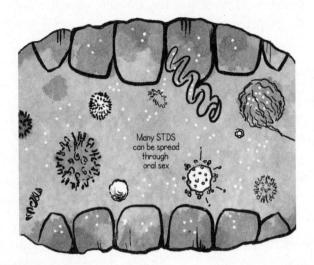

Many STDS can be spread through oral sex

*I*s oral sex generally safer than penetrative intercourse? Absolutely. Can you still transmit STIs through oral sex? Also absolutely. And that includes:

- Chlamydia

- Gonorrhea

- Syphilis

- Herpes

- HPV (human papillomavirus)

- HIV

I know I mentioned avoiding getting semen in your eye because there is a chance of getting ocular herpes, but now I am going to go all sex educator auntie on you. I am from the generation that went into adulthood only to find out sex could kill you.

While that is far less likely to happen nowadays, at least in the Western world thanks to antiretrovirals, Auntie Faith would still prefer you to not have to manage the complexity of an STI.

Firstly, whether using barrier protection or not, don't brush your teeth for two hours before or two hours after oral sex. While your attention to oral hygiene is deeply appreciated, keep to a nice mouthwash gargle, because brushing does create bleeding gums and microabrasions in most of us, and that becomes an entry point for all kinds of cooties.

Now for barrier methods? There is plenty of stuff on the market to help with that. Condoms aren't flavored because vaginas, penises, and anuses like the taste of strawberry!

Along with condoms (both internal and external), we have gloves and finger cots (which can be specifically helpful for oral sex after metoidioplasty), and sex dams. Additionally, a Malaysian gynecologist recently released a condom created from adhesive surgical dressing that can be used in a multitude of ways (innies, outies, and all aroundies). If

you are not in a closed relationship where everyone has been given the all-clear, or have been tested with certain partners and agreed to use barrier protection with others, please please please glove your love. And consider both a pre-exposure prophylaxis (PrEP) to way reduce your risk of getting HIV and post-exposure prophylaxis (PEP) if you aren't taking PrEP and you have a barrier method failure during sexitimes.

One hack that Auntie is cool with? While condoms cannot be DIY'd, sex dams can! Condoms can be cut open (and while you don't want to use a sperimicidal condom for oral sex, you can use one for a dam conversion, so long as the spericidal part isn't where your mouth is going).

Disposable gloves (which make manual sex safer on its own) can also be converted into a dam by cutting off the fingers and then

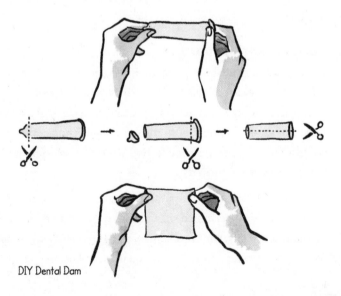

DIY Dental Dam

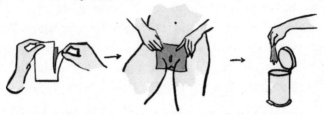

Dental dam
(used on vagina and anus)

cutting open the palm of the glove along one side and unfolding it. But even easier? Saran Wrap as a barrier dam has proven to be effective in the prevention of the spread of STIs. Super easy.

Another trick I picked up from the Scarleteen website about sex dams is to write a non-reversible letter, number, or symbol on one side of the dam so you don't accidentally reverse the dam later during play.

Clean Your Toys Properly

I know, I know...the whole point of having toys is so that you DON'T have to use barrier methods to prevent pregnancy and STIs. But while a toy won't get you pregnant, you can still pass on STIs through toys that were not properly cleaned (not just to and from other people, but even reinfecting yourself with something that had already been treated).

Whether DIY or one you purchased, take good care of your goodies! Don't use a perfumed soap, the ingredients used for scent can irritate your skin. Dr. Bronner's soap is great stuff and comes unscented for sensitive folx. A good quality antibacterial soap is best. You want to wipe them down, not dunk them (unless they are a waterproof toy then dunk away).

Don't put your rubber and plastic type toys in the dishwasher, you can totally melt them. Other than glass toys or stainless steel, you wanna stay away from the dishwasher.

Leather—Wipe down with soap and water or use a special leather cleaner. If the leather comes in contact with bodily fluids, you can disinfect it by wiping it down with a 70% isopropyl rubbing alcohol solution.

Glass—Wash with soap and water

Rubber—if it's something that is going to be inserted, use a condom or dam (see below)...rubber is super porous so they hold bacterial grubbies way too well. Also? Rubber can contain phthalate, which is not something you want seeping into your never-minds (if you wouldn't eat it, don't stick it up anywhere, either).

Silicone—Wash with soap and water

Stainless steel—Wash with soap and water. If you want to be extra about it, stainless steel can go in the dishwasher or can be soaked in a solution of 10:1 water and bleach for ten minutes.

Vinyl and Cyberskin—These are very porous materials that are pretty fragile. These are best washed in warm water and air dried. They can get sticky easily so dusting them with cornstarch is also a good idea (fun fact: corn starch doesn't clump up).

Nylon (paracord is made of nylon, FYI)—Can be washed in the washing machine or by hand with soap and water. You can also remove odor from nylon by soaking it in a solution of water and baking soda.

Fabrics—Wash all fabric as you would fabric you are wearing on your body. Cotton, polyester, and bamboo and the like does fine in a washing machine, silks and wools do better dry cleaned or gently hand washed if you feel confident in managing these materials. Fabric ropes need to be left to be air dried in coils and and stretched occasionally during the drying period so they don't kink up (you are already kinky enough, right, playa?)

Hemp—Hemp can be machine washed on gentle and air dried (it will take 2-5 days to dry completely, so plan accordingly). If you are washing hemp rope, you will want to knot it and and place it in a pillow case before washing (there are lots of videos online with knotting techniques to prepare rope for washing). Hemp rope can be reoiled (baby oil or jojoba oil are good) after drying.

CONCLUSION

Y'all. Y'all? Too much time sitting here trying to figure out how one concludes a book on oral sex. I could make some terrible dad jokes (but already did that). I could be cheerfully encouraging of you getting down with any oral pleasure your heart desires (but already did that, too). And anytime I write anything really insightful and cool in a conclusion, my editor ends up moving it somewhere else in the book and making a whole new conclusion.

Which means I kinda can't win. And yet, this book doesn't go to print without a conclusion (tried that, too).

So I'm going to go with a "thank you" conclusion. I'm writing this last bit after we launched the pre-order and the response has been amazing. So many people are hungry for books of this nature that are practical and comprehensive and full of geekery-science fun. And I deeply appreciate that you trust me with providing that content to you. I talked earlier in this book about culture being anything we create. And I'm so proud of this empowered and inclusive world we are creating together.

See you again soon!

REFERENCES

All That's Interesting. (2019, July 31). A photographic history of the Dildo, one of humanity's most enduring tools. All That's Interesting. Retrieved September 23, 2021, from https://allthatsinteresting.com/history-of-the-dildo.

Banmen, J. (2002). The Satir Model: Yesterday and Today. Contemporary Family Therapy, 24(1), 7-22.

Bansal AS, Chee R, Nagendran V, Warner A, & Hayman G (2007). Dangerous liaison: sexually transmitted allergic reaction to Brazil nuts. Journal of investigational allergology & clinical immunology : official organ of the International Association of Asthmology (INTERASMA) and Sociedad Latinoamericana de Alergia e Inmunologia, 17 (3), 189-91 PMID: 17583107

Basson, Rosemary. (2005). Women's sexual dysfunction: Revised and expanded definitions. CMAJ : Canadian Medical Association journal = journal de l'Association medicale canadienne. 172. 1327-33. 10.1503/cmaj.1020174.

Berman, L., Berman, J., Miles, M., Pollets, D., & Powell, J. A. (2003). Genital self-image as a component of sexual health: relationship between genital self-image, female sexual function, and quality of life measures. Journal of sex & marital therapy, 29 Suppl 1, 11–21. https://doi.org/10.1080/713847124

Blank, J., & Corinne, T. (2011). Femalia. Last Gasp.

Braswell, S. (2015). How the mob introduced Americans to oral sex. Yahoo! Sports. Retrieved October 7, 2021, from http://sports.yahoo.com/news/mob-introduced-americans-oral-sex-080000538.html.

Brice, R. (2019, August 1). U up? how does HRT affect your sex and libido? Healthline. Retrieved October 14, 2021, from healthline.com/health/healthy-sex/hrt-sexuality-libido#4.

Bonham, K. (2013, October 30). *Sexually Transmitted Food allergens*. Scientific American Blog Network. Retrieved November 23, 2021, from https://blogs.scientificamerican.com/food-matters/sexually-transmitted-food-allergens/.   Callen-Lorde. (2021). Pump: Sexual Pleasure & Health Resource Guide for Transmen who

have Sex with Men. Retrieved October 14, 2021, from http://callen-lorde.org/graphics/2021/02/PUMP-TMSM-Health-Guide_Final_V3.2.pdf

Campbell, J. (2020, July 29). Everything we should've grown up knowing about Intersexuality. Volonté. Retrieved October 14, 2021, from lelo.com/blog/intersexuality/.

Centers for Disease Control and Prevention. (2020, September 16). *Disability impacts all of us infographic*. Centers for Disease Control and Prevention. Retrieved November 16, 2021, from cdc.gov/ncbddd/disabilityandhealth/infographic-disability-impacts-all.html#:%7E:text=61%E2%80%8Amillion%E2%80%8Aadults%E2%80%8A

in%E2%80%8Athe%2Chave%E2%80%8Asome%E2%80%8Atype%E2%80%8Aof%E2
%80%8Adisability.

Centers for Disease Control and Prevention. (2020, September 16). *Disability and health overview*. Centers for Disease Control and Prevention. Retrieved November 16, 2021, from cdc.gov/ncbddd/disabilityandhealth/disability.html.

Center for Women's Health. OHSU. (n.d.). Retrieved October 14, 2021, from ohsu.edu/womens-health/benefits-healthy-sex-life.

Chen, A. (2020, September 9). What brain scans tell us about sex. maude. Retrieved October 14, 2021, from https://getmaude.com/blogs/themaudern/on-what-brain-scans-can-tell-us-about-sex.

Engle, G. (2021, November 2). Yes, a perineum orgasm is a real thing-and it's incredible. Men's Health. Retrieved November 16, 2021, from menshealth.com/sex-women/a26782332/perineum-orgasm/.

Ercolano, A. (2021, August 20). FAQ: Phalloplasty: The johns hopkins center for transgender health. FAQ: Phalloplasty | The Johns Hopkins Center for Transgender Health. Retrieved October 15, 2021, from hopkinsmedicine.org/center-transgender-health/services-appointments/faq/phalloplasty.

Fahmy, I., Kamal, A., Metwali, M., Rhodes, C., Mansour, R., Serour, G., & Aboulghar, M. (1999). R-031. vigorous prostatic massage: A simple method to retrieve spermatozoa for ICSI in psychogenic anejaculation. Human Reproduction, 14(Suppl_3), 292–292. https://doi.org/10.1093/humrep/14.suppl_3.292-a

Fellizar, K. (2021, May 25). 12 guys share what oral sex really feels like for them. Bustle. Retrieved October 13, 2021, from bustle.com/wellness/90841-what-do-blow-jobs-feel-like-for-men-12-men-share-what-they-really-think-of.

Foreplay. Foreplay - an overview | ScienceDirect Topics. (n.d.). Retrieved October 13, 2021, from sciencedirect.com/topics/medicine-and-dentistry/foreplay

Fredrick, D. (2002). The Roman Gaze Vision, power and the body. The Johns Hopkins University Press.

Freeman S (1986). Woman allergic to husband's sweat and semen. Contact dermatitis, 14 (2), 110-2 PMID: 3709144

Good, giving, and game: Research confirms that Dan Savage's sex advice works. PsyPost. (2015, April 16). Retrieved September 24, 2021, from psypost.org/2014/10/good-giving-game-research-confirms-dan-savages-sex-advice-works-28965.

Gurza, A. (2016, September 22). Deepthroating while disabled: The symbolism, realities and importance of oral sex to the Queer Cripple. HuffPost. Retrieved September 29, 2021, from huffpost.com/entry/deepthroating-while-disabled-the-symbolism-realities_b_57e3fc80e4b05d3737be5674.

Haber, R. (2002). Virginia Satir: An Integrated, Humanistic Approach. Contemporary

Family Therapy, 24(1), 23-34.

Herbenick, D., & Reece, M. (2010). Development and validation of the female genital self-image scale. The journal of sexual medicine, 7(5), 1822–1830. https://doi.org/10.1111/j.1743-6109.2010.01728.x

Hitchens, C. (2006, October 10). As American as Apple Pie. Vanity Fair. Retrieved October 13, 2021, from vanityfair.com/news/2006/07/hitchens200607.

Hitti, M. (2006, February 22). Men's sex lives better at 50 than 30. WebMD. Retrieved October 20, 2021, from webmd.com/men/news/20060222/mens-sex-lives-better-50-than-30.

Hoffman, M. (n.d.). Chordee: Definition, repair. WebMD. Retrieved October 14, 2021, from webmd.com/men/guide/chordee-repair-treatment.

How to eat out a non-op trans woman. VICE. (n.d.). Retrieved October 14, 2021, from vice.com/en/article/594mak/how-to-eat-out-a-non-op-trans-woman-oral-sex.

How to have a healthy sex life: What to know about orgasms, safety, and your brain. theSkimm. (n.d.). Retrieved October 13, 2021, from theskimm.com/well/healthy-sex-life-guide-WqmsyJtUmknZpUrEAcBIC?utm_source=newsletter_ds&utm_medium=email.

Kasum, M., Orešković, S., Kordić, M., Čehić, E., Hauptman, D., Ejubović, E., Lila, A., & Smolčić, G. (2018). Improvement of Sexual and Reproductive Function in Men with Spinal Cord Lesion. Acta clinica Croatica, 57(1), 149–156. https://doi.org/10.20471/acc.2018.57.01.19

Tina Komarnicky, Shayna Skakoon-Sparling, Robin R. Milhausen & Rebecca Breuer (2019) Genital Self-Image: Associations with Other Domains of Body Image and Sexual Response, Journal of Sex & Marital Therapy, 45:6, 524-537, DOI: 10.1080/0092623X.2019.1586018

Keene, L. C., & Davies, P. H. (1999). Drug-related erectile dysfunction. Adverse drug reactions and toxicological reviews, 18(1), 5–24.

Kessler, A., Sollie, S., Challacombe, B., Briggs, K., & Van Hemelrijck, M. (2019). The global prevalence of erectile dysfunction: A Review. BJU International, 124(4), 587–599. https://doi.org/10.1111/bju.14813

Klein, C., & Gorzalka, B. B. (2009). Sexual functioning in transsexuals following hormone therapy and genital surgery: a review. The journal of sexual medicine, 6(11), 2922–2941. https://doi.org/10.1111/j.1743-6109.2009.01370.x

Knapp, H. (2006). Pornography - The Secret History of Civilisation [DVD]. United ingdom; Koch Vision.

Koelman, C. A., Coumans, A. B., Nijman, H. W., Doxiadis, I. I., Dekker, G. A., & Claas, F. H. (2000). Correlation between oral sex and a low incidence of preeclampsia: a role for soluble HLA in seminal fluid?. Journal of reproductive immunology, 46(2), 155–166. https://doi.org/10.1016/s0165-0378(99)00062-5

Lastella, M., O'Mullan, C., Paterson, J. L., & Reynolds, A. C. (2019). Sex and Sleep: Perceptions of Sex as a Sleep Promoting Behavior in the General Adult Population. Frontiers in public health, 7, 33. https://doi.org/10.3389/fpubh.2019.00033

Lee, B. Y. (2019, March 13). Why a woman suffered an allergic reaction from oral sex. Forbes. Retrieved November 23, 2021, from forbes.com/sites/brucelee/2019/03/12/why-a-woman-had-an-allergic-reaction-after-oral-sex/?sh=4d0e69f341da.

Ley, D. J. (2016). Ethical porn for dicks: A man's guide to responsible viewing pleasure. ThreeL Media.

Liu, H., Shen, S., & Hsieh, N. (2019). A National Dyadic Study of Oral Sex, Relationship Quality, and Well-Being among Older Couples. The journals of gerontology. Series B, Psychological sciences and social sciences, 74(2), 298–308. https://doi.org/10.1093/geronb/gby089

Liu, H., Shen, S., & Hsieh, N. (2018). ORAL SEX FOR OLDER LOVERS: IMPLICATIONS ON RELATIONSHIP QUALITY AND MENTAL HEALTH. Innovation in Aging, 2(Suppl 1), 583. https://doi.org/10.1093/geroni/igy023.2162

Liu, H., Shen, S., & Hsieh, N. (2019, February 20). Oral sex is good for older couples. OUPblog. Retrieved September 29, 2021, from https://blog.oup.com/2019/02/oral-sex-older-couples/.

MailOnline, V. W. for. (2015, January 14). 'Sex toys' dating back 28,000 years made from stone and dried camel dung. Daily Mail Online. Retrieved September 24, 2021, from dailymail.co.uk/sciencetech/article-2908415/The-sex-toys-dating-28-000-years-Ancient-phalluses-stone-dried-camel-dung-started-trend-sex-aids.html.

Marchione, M. (2007, August 22). Sex and the seniors: Survey shows many elderly people remain frisky. The New York Times. Retrieved September 29, 2021, from nytimes.com/2007/08/22/health/22iht-22sex.7216942.html.

Marin, V. (2019, January 24). Why oral sex can trigger anxiety for people with PTSD. Allure. Retrieved October 21, 2021, from allure.com/story/oral-sex-anxiety-after-sexual-assault.

Mayo Foundation for Medical Education and Research. (2021, July 9). Viagra and other erectile dysfunction drugs: Understand how they work. Mayo Clinic. Retrieved October 13, 2021, from mayoclinic.org/diseases-conditions/erectile-dysfunction/in-depth/erectile-dysfunction/art-20047821.

Mayo Foundation for Medical Education and Research. (2019, December 10). Penile implants. Mayo Clinic. Retrieved October 14, 2021, from mayoclinic.org/tests-procedures/penile-implants/about/pac-20384916.

McCabe, M. P., & Taleporos, G. (2003). Sexual esteem, sexual satisfaction, and sexual behavior among people with physical disability. Archives of sexual behavior, 32(4), 359–369. https://doi.org/10.1023/a:1024047100251

Mitrokostas, B. I. (n.d.). *Here's what happens to your body and Brain when you orgasm*. ScienceAlert. Retrieved November 19, 2021, from sciencealert.com/here-s-what-happens-to-your-brain-when-you-orgasm.

Moon, A. (2020). Getting it. Potter/Ten Speed/Harmony/Rodale.

Mor, G., & Cardenas, I. (2010). The immune system in pregnancy: a unique complexity. American journal of reproductive immunology (New York, N.Y. : 1989), 63(6), 425–433. https://doi.org/10.1111/j.1600-0897.2010.00836.x

Muise, A., & Impett, E. A. (2016). Applying theories of communal motivation to sexuality. Social and Personality Psychology Compass, 10(8), 455–467. https://doi.org/10.1111/spc3.12261

Muise, A., & Impett, E. A. (2014). Good, giving, and Game. Social Psychological and Personality Science, 6(2), 164–172. https://doi.org/10.1177/1948550614553641

Nature Publishing Group. (n.d.). Nature news. Retrieved October 20, 2021, from nature.com/scitable/blog/brain-metrics/what_does_fmri_measure/.

Penile implants: The total guide for transsexual men. Trans Health. (2013, May 17). Retrieved October 14, 2021, from trans-health.com/2013/penile-implants-guide/.

Penile implant - top reasons to consider a penile implant. Coloplast Men's Health. (2021, March 16). Retrieved October 14, 2021, from coloplastmenshealth.com/erectile-dysfunction/penile-implants/.

Phallo.net. 2021. Abdominal Phalloplasty - Pedicled Abdominal Flap Phalloplasty. [online] Available at: <phallo.net/procedures/abdominal-phalloplasty.htm> [Accessed 15 October 2021].

Post-traumatic stress, sexual trauma and dissociative ... (n.d.). Retrieved October 21, 2021, from ojp.gov/pdffiles1/Photocopy/153416NCJRS.pdf.

Potenza M. N. (2013). Neurobiology of gambling behaviors. Current opinion in neurobiology, 23(4), 660–667. https://doi.org/10.1016/j.conb.2013.03.004

Rodden, J. (2020, October 8). These medications cause low libido. The Checkup. Retrieved October 20, 2021, from singlecare.com/blog/low-libido-caused-by-medication/.

Robbins SJ, Dauda W, Kokogho A, Ndembi N, Mitchell A, et al. (2020) Oral sex practices among men who have sex with men and transgender women at risk for and living with HIV in Nigeria. PLOS ONE 15(9): e0238745. https://doi.org/10.1371/journal.pone.0238745

Ross, C., & Dodson, B. (2017). Betty Dodson Bodysex basics. Betty A. Dodson Foundation.

Russell, T. (2011). A renegade history of the United States. Free Press.

Sayles, C. (2002). Transformational Change – based on the Model of Virginia Satir. Contemporary Family Therapy, 24(1), 93-109.

Scaccia, A. (2018, September 29). Semen allergy: Symptoms, treatment, effect on fertility, and more. Healthline. Retrieved November 23, 2021, from healthline.com/health/healthy-sex/semen-allergy#causes-and-risk-factors.

Stoya. (2019, September 17). I refuse oral sex from guys for a very good reason. do I owe them an explanation? Slate Magazine. Retrieved October 21, 2021, from https://slate.com/human-interest/2019/09/sex-act-panic-attacks-explanation-sex-advice.html.

Swartz, A. (2021, May 27). A history of oral sex, from Fellatio's ancient roots to the modern blow job. Mic. Retrieved September 24, 2021, from mic.com/p/a-history-of-oral-sex-from-fellatios-ancient-roots-to-the-modern-blow-job-16543812.

Sweeney, E. (2016, June 23). Getting and giving head when you're disabled. Wear Your Voice. Retrieved September 29, 2021, from wearyourvoicemag.com/tips-oral-sex-youre-disabled/.

Talebpour Amiri, F., Nasiry Zarrin Ghabaee, D., Naeimi, R. A., Seyedi, S. J., & Mousavi, S. A. (2016). Aphallia: Report of three cases and literature review. International journal of reproductive biomedicine, 14(4), 279–284.

The Queer Woman's Guide to strap-on blow jobs. VICE. (n.d.). Retrieved October 14, 2021, from vice.com/en/article/vbqzay/strap-on-blow-jobs-queer-women-lesbian-faux-jobs.

Troeller, L., & Schneider, M. (2014). Orgasm: Photographs & interviews. Daylight.

U.S. National Library of Medicine. (n.d.). Drugs that may cause erection problems: Medlineplus Medical Encyclopedia. MedlinePlus. Retrieved October 13, 2021, from https://medlineplus.gov/ency/article/004024.htm.

Vulture. (2008, March 17). How dirty is that Auden poem that was too dirty for the 'times book review'? Vulture. Retrieved October 13, 2021, from vulture.com/2008/03/how_dirty_is_that_auden_poem_t.html.

Waite, L. J., Laumann, E. O., Das, A., & Schumm, L. P. (2009). Sexuality: measures of partnerships, practices, attitudes, and problems in the National Social Life, Health, and Aging Study. The journals of gerontology. Series B, Psychological sciences and social sciences, 64 Suppl 1(Suppl 1), i56–i66. https://doi.org/10.1093/geronb/gbp038

Weiss, S. (2016, May 24). Scientists explain the weird reason why we have oral sex. Glamour. Retrieved October 13, 2021, from glamour.com/story/why-we-have-oral-sex.

Whipple, B., & Komisaruk, B. R. (1985). Elevation of pain threshold by vaginal stimulation in women. Pain, 21(4), 357–367. https://doi.org/10.1016/0304-3959(85)90164-2

What is a substance use disorder? What Is Addiction? (n.d.). Retrieved January 17, 2022, from psychiatry.org/patients-families/addiction/what-is-addiction

Wise, N. J., Frangos, E., & Komisaruk, B. R. (2017). Brain activity unique to orgasm in women: An fmri analysis. The Journal of Sexual Medicine, 14(11), 1380–1391. https://doi.org/10.1016/j.jsxm.2017.08.014

Wright, H., Jenks, R. A., Demeyere, N., Frequent Sexual Activity Predicts Specific Cognitive Abilities in Older Adults, The Journals of Gerontology: Series B, Volume 74, Issue 1, January 2019, Pages 47–51, https://doi.org/10.1093/geronb/gbx065

Yetman, D. (2020, March 5). How common is erectile dysfunction? stats, causes, and treatment. Healthline. Retrieved October 21, 2021, from healthline.com/health/how-common-is-ed#prevalence.

ABOUT THE AUTHOR

Faith Harper PhD, LPC-S, ACS, ACN is a bad-ass, funny lady with a PhD. She's a licensed professional counselor, board supervisor, certified sexologist, and applied clinical nutritionist with a private practice and consulting business in San Antonio, TX. She has been an adjunct professor and a TEDx presenter, and proudly identifies as a woman of color and uppity intersectional feminist. She is the author of dozens of books.

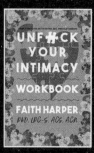

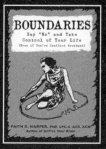

MORE BY DR. FAITH

Books

The Autism Relationships Handbook (with Joe Biel)

Befriend Your Brain

Coping Skills

How to Be Accountable (with Joe Biel)

This Is Your Brain on Depression

Unfuck Your Addiction (with Joseph E Green)

Unfuck Your Adulting

Unfuck Your Anger

Unfuck Your Anxiety

Unfuck Your Blow Jobs

Unfuck Your Body

Unfuck Your Boundaries

Unfuck Your Brain

Unfuck Your Cunnilingus

Unfuck Your Friendships

Unfuck Your Grief

Unfuck Your Intimacy

Unfuck Your Worth

Unfuck Your Writing (with Joe Biel)

Woke Parenting (with Bonnie Scott)

Workbooks

Achieve Your Goals

The Autism Relationships Workbook (with Joe Biel)

How to Be Accountable Workbook (with Joe Biel)

Unfuck Your Anger Workbook

Unfuck Your Anxiety Workbook

Unfuck Your Body Workbook

Unfuck Your Boundaries Workbook

Unfuck Your Intimacy Workbook

Unfuck Your Worth Workbook

Unfuck Your Year

Zines

The Autism Handbook (with Joe Biel)

The Autism Partner Handbook (with Joe Biel)

BDSM FAQ

Dating

Defriending

Detox Your Masculinity (with Aaron Sapp)

Emotional Freedom Technique

Getting Over It

How to Find a Therapist

How to Say No

Indigenous Noms

Relationshipping

The Revolution Won't Forget the Holidays

Self-Compassion

Sex Tools

Sexing Yourself

STI FAQ (with Aaron Sapp)

Surviving

This Is Your Brain on Addiction

This Is Your Brain on Grief

This Is Your Brain on PTSD

Unfuck Your Consent

Unfuck Your Forgiveness

Unfuck Your Mental Health Paradigm

Unfuck Your Sleep

Unfuck Your Work

Vision Boarding

Woke Parenting #1-6 (with Bonnie Scott)

Other

Boundaries Conversation Deck

How Do You Feel Today? (poster)